MW01517080

IMAGINE THIS VALLEY

IMAGINE THIS VALLEY

ESSAYS AND STORIES
CELEBRATING THE
BOW VALLEY

Collected by

Stephen Legault

RMB

RMB | Rocky Mountain Books Ltd.
rmbooks.com
@rmbooks
facebook.com/rmbooks

Cataloguing data available from Library and Archives Canada
ISBN 978-1-77160-176-4 (paperback)
ISBN 978-1-77160-177-1 (electronic)

Printed and bound in Canada by Friesens

Distributed in Canada by Heritage Group Distribution and in the U.S. by Publishers Group West

For information on purchasing bulk quantities of this book, or to obtain media excerpts or invite the author to speak at an event, please visit rmbooks.com and select the "Contact Us" tab.

RMB | Rocky Mountain Books is dedicated to the environment and committed to reducing the destruction of old-growth forests. Our books are produced with respect for the future and consideration for the past.

We acknowledge the financial support of the Government of Canada through the Canada Book Fund and the Canada Council for the Arts, and of the province of British Columbia through the British Columbia Arts Council and the Book Publishing Tax Credit.

Canada

Canada Council Conseil des arts
for the Arts du Canada

BRITISH COLUMBIA

BRITISH COLUMBIA
ARTS COUNCIL
An agency of the Province of British Columbia

To all those past, present and future who
through their creative vision have told a story
to match the splendour of this place.

^ ^ ^

Proceeds from the sale of *Imagine This Valley* will be donated to a fund to support young people in the Bow Valley who wish to pursue a future in writing. Visit www.imaginethisvalley.net to learn more.

CONTENTS

Preface 9 Stephen Legault

PART ONE: A SENSE OF PLACE 13

Bow Corridor 15 Kevin Van Tighem

Yam 27 Ben Gadd

The Business of the River 39 Jon Whyte

My Happy Place, My Home 43 Colette Derworiz

Why We Are So Drawn to the
Magnitude and Beauty of Mountains 51 Ian Brown

The Colour of January 63 Jocey Asnong

Written in My Name 71 Joleen Brewster Niehaus

Exshaw 77 Ruth Oltmann

Downriver 87 Stephen Legault

A Sense of Mountain Place 97 R.W. Sandford

PART TWO: COMING AND GOING 119

The Other Side of Paradise 121 Lynn Martel

Returning to My Senses 143 Jamey Glasnovic

Coffee at the Temple 149 Maria Gregorish

Pulling Up Stakes 157 Rob Alexander

Three Valleys 163 Frances Klatzel

Nothing to Do in the Bow Valley 171 Carol Picard

A Letter from the Bow Valley 177 Michale Lang

PART THREE: THE POLITICS OF PLACE 185

Banff National Park 187 Harvey Locke

The History of a Fantasy 195 Katherine Govier

Banff Kids 211 Miki Kawano

The Nakoda and My
Changing Perspectives 217 John Reilly

The Great Uncertainty 225 Stephen Legault

PART FOUR: THE WILD SIDE 231

Green Eyes on the Goat Creek Trail 233 Kristy Davison

Frozen Redemption 239 Margo Talbot

Searching for the Bow
Valley's Oldest Tree 247 Dustin Lynx

High Peaks and Deep Roots 257 Barry Blanchard

Tributaries 271 Graeme Pole

Conclusion 281 Stephen Legault

Acknowledgments 291

Contributors 293

PREFACE

LAND OF A THOUSAND STORIES

Imagine This Valley is a collaboration of some of the Bow Valley's most talented writers, sharing their passion for, and sometimes struggles with, Alberta's iconic mountain landscape. This idea began in 1996, while I was living in Lake Louise. At the time I was working for Parks Canada in the summer and volunteering for various conservation organizations in the winter. The Banff–Bow Valley Study was underway, and a group of us were advocating for the Bow Valley Wildland through Alberta's Special Places 2000 process, a half-hearted effort by the Alberta government to meet its obligation to conserve 12 per cent of the province's natural landscapes.

And I was writing: mostly ill-tempered letters to the editor, and articles for journals and newspapers and the occasional magazine. The premise for *Imagine This Valley* was that the landscape needed a voice, and that those who love it might come together to tell at least a small part of its story. I pitched the idea to a publisher and got an on-the-fence "write it and we'll have a look" response. That was good enough for me. I approached a dozen or so people, mostly folks with an interest in the Bow Valley's culture and environment, and started to collect essays.

The project got stuck. I didn't have the experience to see it through. The book was abandoned for awhile (about 18 years) until a conversation with RMB's Don Gorman revived it. With a few books under my belt, and two more decades of experience in project management, I decided to restart the undertaking. Some of the old essays, amazingly, were still relevant. New authors were approached. I did my best to collect stories from as many voices in the Bow Valley as I could. In some places – in particular the voices of the First People in the valley – I didn't do so well. I reached out to new immigrants to the valley, and did presentations to high-school students, and got some great writing for the effort. All told, 25 of us pooled our voices for this place we love, struggle with and call home.

The Bow Valley is a land of a thousand stories. People have been coming to this place for more than 10,000 years, and they have brought stories of their own origins and created new ones as they learned to live here or as they just passed through.

Not all of these stories are easy to tell or read. The place looks like paradise, but it's a very human landscape and, as such, has its share of tragedy and challenge. I've encouraged this collection's authors to dig deeply into their own experiences. The result is an unvarnished look at a place and its people. In imagining this valley, we have to consider its challenges as well as triumphs.

Imagine we must. If we're to have any success in creating, in the words of American author Wallace Stegner, "a society to match the scenery," then we will need to employ our hearts and heads in the effort to conceive of a place where our stories equal the vaulted heights of the mountains all around and the deep serenity of the river pulsing at our feet.

Now it's your turn: imagine this valley ...

Stephen Legault, Canmore

PART ONE

A Sense of Place

BOW CORRIDOR

HEART OF A MOUNTAIN ECOSYSTEM

Kevin Van Tighem

Late in June, the Bow Corridor lies sodden beneath heavy, grey clouds. The mountaintops are hidden from view. Rain slants down onto the streets of Canmore and Exshaw, splatters into aspen foliage along the lower slopes of Mount Yamnuska and lashes the face of Lac des Arcs.

It is the kind of day when people stay at home and complain about the weather. The tires of passing trucks and cars on the Trans-Canada Highway hiss and whine. Through the slap-slap of windshield wipers, the travellers peer out at the shining ribbon of asphalt that traces the Bow River Valley west toward the Continental Divide.

Sheets of water pulse across the limestone faces of the Fairholme Range, the Three Sisters and Mount Rundle. Gullies fill with runoff as sparse timberline forests and grassy slopes shed the rain their shallow soils cannot absorb. Cougar and Wind creeks become brown and hungry. The Bow River rises and overflows its channels.

On days like this, the Bow River becomes virtually one with its surrounding landscape. The entire Bow watershed is running water, from the summits of cloud-enshrouded mountains to the rounded gravels of the riverbed below. For just this brief time, running water makes tangible the complex web of living connections that bind the Bow River to the great surrounding mountain ecosystem.

Most people consider the Bow Glacier, on the Continental Divide north of Lake Louise, to be the source of the Bow River. Saying that the Bow begins in the Pacific Ocean, however, would be closer to the truth.

The Pacific Ocean sprawls like an unfathomably vast humidifier between Asia and North America. Earth's rotation on her axis sets winds in motion over the great expanse of sea. The winds sweep east and north across the blue Pacific, drawing immense masses of moisture-laden air up and across the continent where we live.

As air rises, it cools. Since warm air can hold more moisture than cold, rising air masses cool, cloud and shed excess moisture as rain and snow.

Pulled by air ahead and pushed by air behind, the great Pacific weather systems drag bucketing sheets of rain across British Columbia's Coast Mountains. Rolling eastward, the air masses again are forced to rise over the Selkirk and Purcell mountains, where they shed more moisture to grow giant cedars, devil's club and grizzly bears.

Farther inland yet, towns like Cranbrook, Invermere and Golden bask in a balmy rain-shadow climate as the air masses continue to flood eastward. At length they bulge up against the widest, highest mountain mass of all – the Canadian Rockies.

The Bow River is born of the last of that Pacific Ocean moisture, wrung from the weather systems as they spill across the Continental Divide. Bow Glacier receives up to ten metres of snow each year, feeding meltwaters that drain to Bow Lake and thence into the newborn Bow River. The Pipestone River, Healy Creek, Spray River, Ghost and Kananaskis rivers and countless smaller tributaries, each in turn, swell the Bow with its share of the Pacific Ocean's transported wealth.

Anglers fish for brown trout and mountain white-fish in the Bow near Exshaw. Paddlers ease their canoes through the river's riffles below Banff. Children bicycle along riverside trails at Lake Louise. All hear the chatter and murmur of the river. If they could understand its voices, they might hear tales about hidden places high in the Rockies where the headwaters rise, and rumours of the great global forces that sustain the river and its landscapes.

There was a time, only a few thousands of years ago, when snow fell more heavily on the high country and melted more slowly. For millennia, immense glaciers filled the valleys of the Bow and its tributaries, flowing slowly eastward. Rivers of ice carved out the valleys that hold today's more modest river flows. The glaciers steepened valley walls, flattened the valley floors, and left behind complex landscape patterns when at last – starting about 15,000 years ago – they melted back. Their dwindling remnants survive today in cold, sheltered refuges high in the mountains of Banff National Park but may be gone completely within a few more decades.

Free of ice at last, the Bow Corridor began to evolve into today's rich ecological mosaic. Plants and animals that had survived the frozen millennia west of the Rockies began to spread east through Kicking Horse, Vermilion and Kananaskis passes. Prairie vegetation crept in from refugia south of the ice. Northern wildlife appeared from the east.

Along the Bow Corridor, glacial terraces, limestone mountains, valley-bottom springs and a mild, low-elevation climate uncommon in the Rocky Mountains offered new opportunities for life. Plants and animals that had evolved separately, in very different regions, encountered one another in the raw new landscape. A unique ecological complex evolved.

Thousands of people now live in or visit the Bow Corridor, but few spend much time contemplating the origins of the river, its landscape and the ecological complexity they sustain. We live in the present, for the most part, and plan for the future. Our focus is too often on development and change rather than history and continuity.

Nonetheless, unravelling the rich and revealing ecology of the Bow Corridor is a valuable exercise in fascination and humility. One could argue that no human plans for the Bow Corridor can have any ecological or ethical validity unless they are founded upon a sombre consideration of the relationships, processes and living complexity that give the place its history, its vitality and its identity.

We Albertans are proud of our chinooks – warm winds that sweep down from the Rocky Mountains and turn the prairie winter into short-lived springtime. The Bow Corridor, from Banff all the way east beyond Calgary, is a funnel for those chinook winds. The chinook, in fact, is all that remains of those great Pacific weather systems that leave so much snow in the high country. Depleted of moisture and warmed by their sudden descent to low elevations, the winds repeatedly sweep winter snow from south and west exposures.

Their mild winter climate and balmy summers make low-elevation valleys and hillsides along the Bow Corridor exceptionally valuable. The cooler, heavily forested landscapes more typical of the Canadian Rockies sustain far less diversity and abundance of life. The montane ecoregion – as ecologists describe this landscape of mixed grassland, aspen thickets and forests of Douglas fir and lodgepole pine – exists in only a few other parts of Alberta.

Up to 1,300 elk spend each winter in the montane, avoiding the deep snows of the high country winter. Bighorn sheep, mule deer and other large animals also congregate on montane winter ranges. Here they can count on abundant grass, shallow snow and the occasional spell of mild weather.

Banff National Park's famous elk herds do not winter

along the Bow Corridor by chance or coincidence. They are here because in all the cold, inhospitable northern Rockies, this is one place where they can generally be sure of surviving the winter.

The sunny south-facing Benchlands above Canmore and the windblown ridges of Grotto and Pigeon mountains and Wind Ridge are vital to populations of elk, bighorn sheep and mule deer that range much farther afield each summer. If someone were to take away those winter ranges, a vast expanse of the southern Alberta Rockies would become ecologically impoverished.

Wolves and other large carnivores are just as dependent on the montane ecoregion and the Bow Corridor's windy ridges and slopes. Their fate is tied to that of the large grazing animals they eat. A rabies scare in the 1950s led the government to poison all the wolves south of Jasper National Park. It took until the late 1970s before single wolves and small packs reappeared in Banff National Park. They had spread southward from the still-wild northern forests of Alberta.

Today, wolves continue to colonize their ancestral ranges. Wolves from the Bow Valley have wandered as far south as Idaho and Wyoming. A major highway and railroad traverse the Bow Corridor, however, and the valley is subject to increasing development pressures outside the national park. In all the Rocky Mountains, this narrow band of human activity and fragmented habitat remains the most challenging obstacle for large carnivores like the wolf.

The single biggest killer of wolves in Banff National Park, according to wildlife biologist Paul Paquet, is the

Trans-Canada Highway. Fencing the highway and providing crossing structures may change that, but the growing number of humans and dogs running wild across the surrounding slopes displaces wolves to poorer habitat, where they can at least avoid conflict. As roads and development fragment montane valley bottoms, wolves and other large carnivores – never common at the best of times – face ever-greater risk of disturbance and displacement.

Dr. Paquet helped Parks Canada and Canmore-area land planners identify key movement corridors for wolves, cougars and bears that, if protected, may help these scarce animals avoid becoming separated into small, isolated populations. One such corridor extends from the Bow Valley through the Spray Lakes area into southern BC and Peter Lougheed Provincial Park. Another runs through the Wind Creek Valley/Skogan Pass area into Kananaskis Country. Both help wolves and other wildlife maintain essential genetic links between northern populations and those farther south.

For those who live in or visit the Bow Corridor, a chance sighting of a wolf loping along the Bow River floodplain or a herd of elk grazing on the Benchlands north of Canmore is something to savour and talk about. It is part of a unique quality of experience that this montane area offers. But it is also a reminder of the complex links that connect landscape, climate and wildlife populations within what Paul Paquet and other scientists call the Central Rockies Ecosystem – an ecosystem whose heart is the Bow Corridor.

Ecosystems, of course, involve more than just the

large animals. From the cordilleran flycatcher to the brown thrasher, from bull trout to wolverine, and from limber pine to sparrow's egg orchid, the Bow Corridor is a rich mix of prairie, western, alpine and northern plants and animals. The most sensitive elements of the ecosystem are often the least known.

Long-toed salamanders, for example, are among the few amphibians that can thrive in the Rockies. Even so, only the gentle climate of the montane ecoregion suits this dark little salamander. Even there, its lifestyle confines it to a few specialized habitats.

Salamanders venture out of their homes in the soil and rotting logs of aspen forests, willow thickets and other montane habitats each May. They follow their instincts overland, back to the ponds of their birth. There they mate, then lay their eggs in shallow water. The spring sun warms the eggs until tiny black larvae, like little tadpoles, hatch out.

Long-toed salamanders were once widespread, but many populations have fallen victim to the changes that the 20th century brought to the Bow Corridor. National park wardens and provincial fisheries officers unwittingly helped to exterminate some populations by stocking small lakes and ponds with trout. Long-toed salamander larvae are easy prey for these predators. Dr. Geoff Holroyd of the Canadian Wildlife Service points out that Pilot Pond, in Banff National Park, was once known as Lizard Lake because of its salamander population. Trout stocking eliminated them.

In other parts of the Bow Corridor, roads block salamander migration routes. Wetland filling and gravel quarrying have eliminated breeding ponds. Long-toed salamanders are invisible and unknown to most of the people whose activities have changed their ecosystems. Consequently, they now survive in only a few ponds and wetlands along the Bow Corridor. These few vulnerable populations still make their annual journeys each May, unaware of mounting development pressures and land-use changes that threaten their future.

Mountain landscapes contain a great deal of ecological complexity. Their rugged terrain produces complex interplays among slope aspect, sunshine, drainage and wind. South-facing slopes receive more sun and wind than those that face north. As a result, southern exposures often have dry grassland, aspen forest and open Douglas fir forests. Denser forests of pine and spruce clothe north-facing slopes. Down along the river, where spring floods rearrange the floodplain year after year, thickets of water-loving willows and red-osier dogwoods alternate with rich old forests of spruce and balsam poplar. Rushes, dryas and mountain fireweed cover newly exposed river flats.

Geoff Holroyd's studies of wildlife populations in Banff National Park showed that the montane ecoregion has by far the greatest density and diversity of wildlife in the Rockies. Alluvial fans – fan-shaped landforms where tributary streams enter the main Bow Valley – are among the most important habitats because of their poplar forests, rich soils and available water. Unfortunately, they are also the most desirable for development. Most Banff National Park campgrounds and tourist lodges, not to mention the entire towns of Banff and

Exshaw, most of Canmore and the Dead Man's Flats service area, occupy montane alluvial fans. Ironically, these ecologically productive sites continue to be subject to the same kind of debris-laden floods that built them; any development there is at risk from catastrophic flooding. Bad land-use planning has its own karma.

Other ecologically important habitats include grassland areas, the floodplain of the Bow River and its tributaries, old-growth Douglas fir forests, and areas of calcium-rich springs.

Some early land-use changes actually increased the ecological diversity of the Bow Corridor. Introduced rhubarb and pasture grasses colonized the slack heaps that resulted from early coal mines. Road clearing brought new weeds and exotic plants, some of which proved palatable to elk and small rodents. Park wardens and provincial fisheries staff added new species of fish – rainbow, brown and brook trout – to rivers and streams.

With each change, however, the Bow Corridor became a little different from what it had been when the Peigan, Ktunaxa and Stoney people had it to themselves. The unprecedented arrival of roads, bulldozers, exotic weeds and mortgages abruptly interrupted the long, gradual evolution that had been taking place ever since the retreat of the glaciers.

A century later, the Bow Corridor's scenic beauty camouflages the degree to which incremental change has compromised its ecosystem. Wolves are rare, otters and fishers extinct and even elk appear unable to rebuild their populations outside Banff National Park. Grizzly bears seldom roam the Bow River's floodplain and, Paul Paquet warns, could disappear within a decade or two. Long-toed salamanders survive in only a few ponds. Most ecologically significant areas in the corridor – places like Wind Valley, the Canmore Benchlands, Yamnuska and Grotto Mountain – now appear on the blueprints and plans of resort developers and mining companies.

"One of the penalties of an ecological education," American conservationist Aldo Leopold wrote half a century ago, "is that one lives alone in a world of wounds."

Human populations have mushroomed in the Bow Corridor over the past century; nobody can be said to live alone there now. Even so, few are conscious of the extent of the ecosystem's wounds.

Many of those wounds can, to some degree, be healed. Most are products of ignorance, inflicted by generations of Albertans whose optimism and ambitions exceeded their ecological knowledge. Understanding and knowledge, at least among a growing minority, has increased in recent years.

Ecological restoration – and the protection of the still-considerable ecological wealth that survives in the Bow Corridor and its surrounding mountain ecosystem – will not be easy. In part, they will depend on widespread knowledge of how the greater ecosystem works. They will also require a strong community commitment to sustaining the ecological diversity that makes the Bow Corridor so rich and unique a place.

Perhaps most important, the survival of the Bow Corridor's ecological integrity will require that thousands of human beings who now feel a personal stake

in the Bow Corridor recognize that ecological principles apply to humans too. Just as the Bow ecosystem
can never support more than a few hundred elk or a few
dozen wolves, there is also a finite limit on how much
human activity and development it can sustain.

YAM

Ben Gadd

Not as in "sweet potato." This Yam is a block of limestone, a mountain-sized block. But like the yam of Africa, it is tasty indeed, a chunk of the Canadian Rockies sweet beyond compare. Tangy, too, when you're hanging from it by your fingertips.

"Yam" is short for Yamnuska, pronounced "Yam-NUSS-ka." This is not the official name of the mountain. The official name is Mount Laurie (Îyâmnathka). "Yamnuska Mountain," which I frequently see in print, is incorrect.

"Îyâmnathka" is a First Nations word that means "flat-faced mountain." The name is pronounced pretty much the way it is spelled, i.e., rather like "Yamnuska." "Îyâmnathka" was applied to the peak by the Stoney Nakoda people, who arrived in the Rockies in the 1700s. Part of the Great Sioux Nation of Minnesota, Manitoba and Ontario, the Nakodas had fled westward from all things non-Sioux, which were killing them.

"Stoney," spelled "–ey" instead of "–y," is an Anglophone tag alluding to the Sioux method of boiling meat by putting hot stones into a bag of broth.

I'm guessing that the Stoney Nakodas gave Îyâmnathka its name within five minutes of seeing it for the first time. Yamnuska stands out – look northward from the Trans-Canada Highway as you approach the mountain front – and the south face is as flat as they come. It's as if someone wielding a huge cleaver had whacked the mountain down the middle, then called upon a goodly team of glaciers to carry half away.

In truth, glaciers did remove much of Yamnuska, and on the north, west and east sides, as well as the south side. It took most of the ice ages to do it, meaning about two million years.

Yamnuska overlooks a grassy, windy, glacial-outwash plain along the Bow River. The local name for this place is "Morley Flats." Here the Bearspaw, Chiniki and Wesley bands of Stoney Nakodas have their official reserve. It dates to 1877, when southern Alberta's famous Treaty No. 7 was signed.

Central to that reserve is the village of Morley, also known as "Morleyville." The name honours William Morley Punshon, a renowned English Methodist minister who spent five years in Canada but never seems to have visited the Rockies. However, Rev. Punshon did make it possible for Rev. George McDougall to set up shop there in 1873.

Nothing unusual about that. Canadian First Nations were commonly beset, er, *served* by Christian missionaries. George McDougall was obliged to support the prevailing government attitude toward "Indians," which was patronizing and oppressive. But McDougall also seems to have done much to ease his parishioners' painful transition from a proud, free life of hunting and gathering to a hemmed-in, rule-bound and dependent existence on the reserve.

In that same vein, we have the story of Yamnuska's other appellation, Mount Laurie.

John Laurie was a Calgary high-school teacher. He's the person for whom the city's John Laurie Boulevard is named. Born in Ontario in 1901, Laurie met the Stoneys in the 1930s, liked them and soon became an advocate for them in matters educational and legal. He documented their language and practices, made audio recordings, took many photos and wrote books and stories about them, including 62 articles for *Western Cattleman* magazine.

Laurie was a prominent member of the Alberta Indian Association, for which he volunteered as secretary for 15 years. Laurie and Calgary lawyer Ruth Gorman won full and unrestricted federal voting rights for all of Canada's First Nations people, a major accomplishment. In 1940 Laurie was ceremonially adopted by Enos Hunter, chief of the Wesley Band, as a son named White Cloud. This made him a Stoney Nakoda.

After John Laurie's death in 1959, Îyâmnathka/Yamnuska received the official name "Laurie, Mount." This was fine with the Stoneys, who loved John Laurie, but Laurie himself would surely have objected to dispensing with the Sioux name. In 1984 this error was put right when the Geographic Names Board of Canada amended the name to its present "Mount Laurie (Îyâmnathka)."

"Yamnuska" remains an unofficial name. Should it, too, be added? Nay; the label already takes nearly as much space on the map as does the mountain itself.

Reaching the summit, elevation 2235 metres above sea level, is not difficult. Trails pioneered by bighorn sheep make for an easy ascent. I'll bet the first human to reach the top was a Clovis hunter after those sheep, 10,000 years ago.

The Stoney Nakodas must have got there long before kids from nearby Camp Chief Hector began hiking up with their adult leaders in the 1930s. A dangerous spot along the trail—the "Very Scary Traverse," aptly named—was rendered harmless in 2002 by the addition of a steel cable to hang onto. In 2011 the unofficial cable was replaced by a government-installed chain.

Yam's precipitous south face remained unclimbed until the 1950s. Before then, mountaineers capable of scaling the thousand-foot cliff must have walked along the base, necks bent way back as they scanned the cracks and corners for a way up. Perhaps a few of them broke out the rope and gave it a go. If they did, though, they seem to have retreated, intimidated.

Not so Austrian mountaineers Hans Gmoser and Leo Grillmair, who discovered Yam soon after arriving in Canada together in 1951. On November 23, 1952, they and English physiotherapist Isabel Spreat made the first ascent of the south face.

It was a very bold climb, completed in one effort. The unseasonably warm day began with seven climbers, most of them members of the Alpine Club of Canada, roping up at the start of the cliff's easiest-looking line. The idea was to explore, not necessarily to make a serious attempt. Everyone but Grillmair, Gmoser and Spreat backed off. The three continued, equipped with only a single rope and no pitons or carabiners. Grillmair, who had been laid up for months with a broken leg, was wearing his street shoes. No matter; he was a fine climber and very keen. He went first most of the way, on the "sharp end" of the rope, as the Scots refer to the inherent danger of leading. Gmoser recalls climbing in ski boots that day. Spreat was the only one with proper footwear. She had on mountaineering boots with grippy Vibram rubber soles.

Late in the afternoon, the would-be first-ascensionists had nearly reached the top. The climbing had not been difficult, except for one especially steep bit that Grillmair had overcome in fine style. But now they stood before an ominous-looking vertical crack. It was wide, deep and dark, a most unwelcome surprise.

Yet it was clearly the only way up. Retreat at this point would have been very risky. The temperature was dropping and snow was beginning to fall. They had to get off the mountain, and soon.

Leo Grillmair moved into the crack, arms and legs stretched between the two walls. The holds were few, and the rock, while not wet, had a disconcerting slipperiness. Taking extraordinary care, Grillmair worked his way up and out of sight. Just before he ran out of rope, he came to a good stopping point and belayed Spreat and Gmoser safely up to him. Above, the crack seemed to close off in the gloom. Would he have to somehow climb back out to the lip and finish the route by struggling up overhanging rock with a lot of air under his feet and no pitons in place for safety?

Not a pleasant prospect. So Grillmair chose to jam his way directly upward between the narrowing walls. And then he saw it: daylight ahead. A few moves higher he stuck his head up through a hole – a hole set back from the edge of the cliff! – and climbed out onto the crest of the mountain. The hikers' trail lay only metres away.

Thus was Yam's most famous gift bestowed upon three worried climbers who were very happy to receive it. Many others have since been similarly delighted as they have enjoyed the weird and wonderful finish to the route that was soon named "Grillmair Chimneys."

Grillmair had shown that the south face of Yam was climbable. Inviting, even. Yam was made of reasonably solid Cambrian limestone in a mountain range known for its rottenness. The south face was a mile long, offering many enticing route possibilities. The peak was only an hour's drive west of Calgary, plus a 45-minute hike to the foot of the cliff. This was a short approach by Canadian Rockies standards. When the Calgary Mountain Club was founded in 1960, Yam quickly became a favourite place to go.

The earlier routes on Yam have the sort of descriptive names that rock climbers of that era liked to confer. In addition to "Grillmair Chimneys," you'll see "King's Chimney," "Windy Slabs," "Calgary Route," "Direttissima" (a direct line to the summit), "Forbidden Corner," "Chockstone Corner," "The Bowl" and "Yellow Edge."

When J.R.R. Tolkien's novels became popular in the

1970s, Yam climbers borrowed from his books to name "Lord of the Rings," "Necromancer," "Balrog," "Gollum Grooves" and "Grond." "Gormenghast" is from the fantasy novels of Mervyn Peake.

Some names are hip: "Freak Out," "Dazed and Confused," "Rocket Man," "Astro Yam." Other names are double entendres or puns: "Missionary's Crack," "General Pain," "It's all McConnell's Fault" (the McConnell Fault is an important geological feature of the mountain). Yamnuska may be one of the few mountains in the world to have a route named "Unnamed." There's a route named for me ("Ben's") and another that comes from one of my books ("Corvus Corax").

I first saw Yam in 1968, when I was a 22-year-old climber newly arrived in Calgary from the mountains of Colorado. I was greatly impressed. So was my younger brother Morgan, both of us riding along in my 1957 Volkswagen microbus. Having escaped from the war-crazed United States, we were pleased to find that the Canadian Rockies equalled or bettered anything we had seen in the American Rockies, especially so since we were going to be unable to return home for some time.

The late-afternoon angle of the sun was perfect for marking out every feature of Yam's south face in contrasting brightness and shadow. I remember pointing out a sweeping crescent-shaped crack that ran all the way up the cliff from base to top. I asked my brother, who was a more experienced rock climber than I, whether it looked to him to be a proper chimney, wide enough to admit the full human body, or whether it was a hand-width crack. He squinted over to the peak, which we assumed to be perhaps a half mile off and about a hundred metres high, and allowed that it might be an "off-width" crack, the sort of thing that's too wide to jam an arm or a leg into, but also too narrow to get inside and chimney up. Morgan thought it would be difficult to climb.

The following summer I was 200 metres up Grillmair Chimneys – the "crack" we had seen – which was actually more than five and a half kilometres from the highway and wide enough to swallow my microbus. We had no knowledge of the route. If Morgan had been along, he would have wormed his way back into the chimney as Leo Grillmair had done, leading us to the climb's sensational conclusion. But Morgan was not along, and the fellow I was climbing with was no better a route-finder than I. We were both so intimidated by that black, gaping gash in the mountain that we chose to force our way up beside it, terrified on very steep rock that refused to admit our pitons and promised us a long fall if we slipped.

Yam was not like back home in Colorado. Yam was an order of magnitude bigger and more committing. In the moth-and-flame manner that climbers know so well, Yam was way more attractive.

I came back to Yamnuska's great south face over and over, year after year. I learned how close to approach the flame, savouring the adrenalin as I climbed high above my last piton or tiptoed across a thin traverse to a blind corner that might or might not lead to climbable rock beyond. The thickening clouds streaming over the top of the cliff might or might not bring lightning on the summit. After a few years I came to love Yamnuska.

In exchange, Yam didn't kill me.

In fact, it tolerated my whole family. One June afternoon, my wife and I took our two little boys with us as we walked along the trail up Yamnuska's east ridge to a flat spot from which we could witness the summer solstice. There we lay in our sleeping bags, the wind rearranging our hair from different directions through the night as we watched that quintessentially Canadian band of boreal light move along the northern horizon. We returned to do this year after year, sometimes getting chased off the mountain at three a.m. by a thunderstorm.

The Gadds grew ten years older against Yamnuska's millions. We moved to Jasper, far from Yam, and I seldom returned to climb it. As a Parks Canada naturalist paid to explain the geology of the Rockies, I spent my summer evenings onstage in national park campgrounds, telling the visitors that the limestone around them originated hundreds of millions of years ago in the sea. Microscopic crystals of calcite would form inside the cells of planktonic cyanobacteria. Those cells would pop open, and the lime would drift down onto the Paleozoic seabed. Strange animals were crawling about in the deepening ooze. I had no idea what those creatures looked like, because their bodies were too soft to leave fossils, but I did know from examining the wavy, churned-up character of the layers that every crystal of calcite in them had passed through the gut of one marine organism or another. Thus came the realization that Yamnuska's awesome scarp, golden and dignified in an Alberta sunset, was basically 300 metres of accumulated fish poop.

Perspective having been gained, a further visit to Yamnuska produced something quite different from a new climbing route or a new bit of scientific insight. It produced a novel about ravens.

Yamnuska is famous for ravens. The big, black birds have a way of soaring by climbers and cheerfully saying "Awk!" Is it encouragement? Are they laughing at us? Are they hoping we'll fall off so they can pluck out our eyeballs as the Twa Corbies did when they found that newly slain knight? Who knows?

Whatever, I decided to write a story about the mountain and its resident flock. For three days in the summer of 1989 I perched in various aeries on Yam's east end, watching the ravens. They did interesting things, which I wrote down. At the end of the third day I read all the notes and pondered them into a plot.

McClelland & Stewart published *Raven's End* in 2001. Since then, thousands of Canadian readers have discovered Yamnuska—the Yamnuska I knew, complete with climbers and corvids and pikas and a weasel named "Optimistic Molt." Thousands of additional readers in Italy, Germany, Holland, Denmark and Japan have found themselves in armchair flight over the Yam as publishers in those countries have brought out translated editions in which the ravens say "ouk!" or "ork!" or "owk!" or "årk!" or 「オーク！」 instead of "awk!"

Yamnuska, the Yam, Îyâmnathka, Mount Laurie ... whatever you call it, this mountain is worth seeing, worth visiting on foot, worth protecting from the cancerous quarrying going on at its base or the inevitable touristy tramway to the top that some corporation is bound to propose. Pick an autumn morning, when the aspen groves of the foothills are brilliantly yellow against the deep green of the conifers. If you're driving from Calgary, take Highway 1A, not the Trans-Canada, so you approach the mountain from the proper angle. When you get to the bridge over Old Fort Creek, Yamnuska will look like a round castle set high on a hill. Pull over and stop. You may see a few black flecks circling up there – ravens soaring in the first thermals of the day – and they will provide the true scale of the scene. It's big. It's old. It's going to outlast us, no matter how much of the world we reduce to dollars and dust.

THE BUSINESS OF THE RIVER

Jon Whyte

The business of the river is one of Banff's sustaining pleasures. I suppose I have looked upon the Bow now for 30 or more summers and have always found it to be among the most pleasing of rivers. The only other river I have spent any time beside is the North Saskatchewan as it passes through Edmonton, a decently powerful river but not as sustainingly pleasant as the Bow.

It used to be that on the portion of the river path between Caribou and Wolf streets there were three places where the path divided into two parts, narrowing down and separating to go on either side of a tree or two trees. It was always our belief that those parts of the path had been designated with bears in mind.

"What would you do if you were walking beside the river and you met a bear?"

"I'd go on one side of the path and the bear would go on the other."

The designers or makers of the trail had that very instance in mind. The bear would walk on one side of the tree – or trees – and we would walk on the other. Path designers are very clever. But in all these years of walking beside the river, even in the days when bears were more common in the town, I cannot recall ever having to test the possibility. Now, of course, there are fewer bears in town, and the small islands of trees are gone from the path, so it is impossible to test the foresight of the path's makers.

Since the Bow to me is all rivers – Saskatchewan, Nile, Amur and Lena – all other rivers I judge by the Bow, a tough standard. The Ganges can never be so beautifully green as the Bow; for all rivers must be judged by their greenness, the Bow being so beautifully coloured. The Amur, as we saw it at Khabarovsk, is too wide; a river should not be so wide that its other bank seems not to be part of the river.

The Mississippi, which I know only from Minneapolis–Saint Paul, is too narrow a river, and does not have forest on its far shore, nor sweepers to increase its graciousness. The Ottawa in flood is too tormented, huge and dangerous. The South Saskatchewan in Medicine Hat flows between hills that are too soft.

But the Bow at Banff is properly wide, wild, shored, and green, gracious, soft and swift. It would be difficult to find any other river anywhere that sustains itself so riverly.

I remember a comment passed on to me at second

hand, a comment from a Swiss girl who compared our river to hers, and she was much attracted by the sweepers of the river, those trees that lean and incline to the water as the bank on which they live is undercut by the current. Those trees, she said, they make the river so Canadian.

Pressed for an explanation, she went on to say that in Europe the rivers are all employed for commerce, and any trees that might grow on their banks must be cut down. A tree could never be allowed to grow out and impede the way of business.

But the business of the Bow is just to flow and be beautiful, and it does its business surpassingly well. It stays just the right width, and it turns the right green when the runoff is over and summer is cresting.

It fails to flood with the excess it used to, and we no longer find drowned birds on its shore among the shooting stars, but a few forest fires will get it back to its old violence.

And it continues to be the right and proper place in Banff to get away from the rick and rattle of Banff Avenue. As one stands on the new shore now, the far shore seems to be a threshold of the wild world. The river restores balance.

MY HAPPY PLACE, MY HOME

Colette Derworiz

I always wanted to hike Ha Ling Peak. Whenever I looked up at it, I wondered what it would be like to see the Bow Valley from 2400 metres.

Even its history intrigued me. As the story goes, a Chinese cook for Canadian Pacific Railway accepted a $50 bet that he couldn't climb the peak in less than ten hours. He started at seven a.m. on October 24, 1896, and was back in time for lunch.

No one believed him so he did it again, this time taking some of those who doubted him along and planting a large flag at the summit that could be seen from the town of Canmore.

The mountain was named Chinaman's Peak in his honour, but it was later changed to Ha Ling to be more politically correct.

I heard the story many times and gazed up at the

peak every time I drove by, wondering if I would ever make it up there.

In the summer of 2012, more than a decade after moving to Alberta, I finally trudged up the 700 metres to the historic summit with some friends. We stopped to catch our breath partway up, but it didn't take ten hours.

Not even close – and the top was even better than I had imagined.

Perhaps it's appropriate that the same peak provided one of my life's "ah-ha" moments a year or so later – it was my second trip up.

In September 2013, my childhood friend Ryan sent a text to ask if I knew anyone who might want to rent the suite in his house in Canmore.

"I might," I quipped, adding a disclaimer that I had just returned from a four-day backcountry trip to Mount Assiniboine – one that involved a 27-kilometre hike over a mountain pass to both get in and come out. I was exhausted so might be a little delirious, I wrote.

"We'd love to have you, with your delirium and all," he replied.

Maybe it wasn't such a crazy idea.

I work in Calgary, but I heard more and more over the years about people who regularly drive the hour-long commute to the city.

A conversation with my editor-in-chief at the *Calgary Herald* made it clear that it wasn't necessary for me to be working in the office every day.

"You could live in Timbuktu," he said, quickly adding, "as long as you're writing."

This idea could actually work.

I was already travelling to the Bow Valley several times a week, whether for my work as the environment writer for the newspaper or to play in the mountains on the weekends.

Maybe it was time to make a move.

The decision was solidified a few weeks later on that second, somewhat easier (now that I knew what to expect) hike up Ha Ling.

As a friend and I sat at the summit after an invigorating climb, it dawned on me: this is my happy place.

Yet some questions lingered. Is it my happy place because it's a getaway from the city, an escape from daily deadlines and a way-too-busy schedule? Or would the day-to-day pressures simply follow me there?

It's not like I was unhappy in Calgary, but it had certainly gotten hectic in recent years. I lived downtown, where daily congestion has become a way of life. The commute to work was growing longer and more frustrating. Even on weekends, driving out of downtown meant navigating through a maze of construction.

Life there had also gotten heavier in recent years.

In late 2009, I lost two of my best friends. In September, a ten-year relationship with my then-boyfriend came to an abrupt end. Three months later, my close friend Michelle Lang was killed while reporting for our newspaper in Afghanistan.

The day before she died, she emailed to give me a pep talk on how to deal with an upcoming post-break-up talk with the ex.

It never happened, because of the life-altering news

that same day. On December 30, Michelle and four soldiers were killed by a roadside bomb as they travelled back to the base from an Afghan village. Her death was a shocking end to an already rough year.

In the days that followed, some friends and I travelled through a haze to Trenton, Ontario, for a repatriation ceremony to welcome Michelle back on Canadian soil; to Vancouver, where she would be buried near her childhood home; and back to Calgary for another public memorial.

For the next few months, it wasn't always clear what I was grieving. All I knew was that my heart was broken. It actually ached.

I mourned the death of my friend, who was the first Canadian journalist to die covering the war in Afghanistan. She went over, as many friends had, to document the war. The difference was that she didn't come home alive. It meant she didn't get married six months later; didn't get a chance to have children.

It made me acutely aware of my own situation: newly single in my mid-30s, bringing up questions of whether I'd ever marry or have my own children. I suppose I mourned that, too.

Those questions linger, but I've learned to make the best of whatever life hands me – including the chance to live in the Bow Valley.

The Rocky Mountains have always held a special place in my heart.

As a child, I remember driving through Banff National Park on the way to visit my grandparents on Vancouver Island. It was so different than life on the farm in

Saskatchewan, mostly flat prairies smattered with small valleys and rolling hillsides.

The mountains, towering above as we drove by, screamed of adventure. As a teenager, I remember skiing in the Rockies for the first time with my family. It was scary, but it challenged me.

Perhaps that's it.

Thoughts of the mountains followed me through life as I finished high school, travelled to Ottawa then Regina to earn two degrees and landed my first full-time journalism job at the *Herald*. Given a choice between Regina, Edmonton and Calgary, I picked Calgary – mostly because of its closeness to the mountains.

During the next 14 years, I worked hard and made friends who became like family. We headed west every time we had a chance to hike or ski.

It wasn't until the last five years that I realized how important those trips had become. They provided peace of mind. It sounds clichéd, but it's often where I escaped to think.

A wander along the Bow River or a hike up one of the many mountains – Ha Ling, Castle or even Tunnel – helped to provide clarity. With the city feeling more crowded, a day in the mountains always soothed my soul. It helped me breathe again, sleep better.

Over time, the haze lifted.

Life became comfortable again – although the comforts of home still held strong memories.

I remembered the exact spot where I sat the day my relationship ended. A couple of days later, as Michelle and I walked out of work, she sensed something was wrong. Before the first tear fell, she called her fiancé and dropped everything to follow me home. I remembered where she hugged me and told me everything would be okay.

A few months later, I wasn't far from that spot when I found out she was killed in Afghanistan.

So there were a lot of memories in that apartment in downtown Calgary.

It was time for a fresh start, a change of scenery. And, if you're going to change the scenery, there's no better place than the heart of the Rockies.

I moved to Canmore on a warm October day, taking the evening to go for a walk up a ridge that overlooks the small but bustling mountain town.

As I wondered whether I had made the right decision, the sun began to set behind the mountains, lighting up the entire sky in a brilliant orange glow. It felt right.

After two years of living in the Bow Valley, it still feels right. Right, but not always perfect. I commute to Calgary a couple of times a week, which can come with white-knuckle drives through wind, rain or snow.

I sometimes miss the comforts – and memories – in Calgary, a city I called home for as long as I lived on my family's farm. I miss quick jaunts up Douglas Fir Trail and runs or bikes along the Bow River pathway, which would sometimes end at a friend's house for a glass of wine. It's more difficult to spend quality time with those friends, the ones who've become like my second family. We've made it work, though, and I've made more friends in Canmore.

So it's pretty close to perfect.

I can see the peaks of Three Sisters from the comforts of my couch, where I often work. I can go for a run or a hike after work and feel the stress wash away as soon as I take in that first breath of mountain air. And I'm never too far from Ha Ling – one of the mountains that have intrigued, inspired and, ultimately, brought clarity at a time when I needed it most.

So, can your happy place be your home?

Time will ultimately tell, but whether I live in Canmore or Calgary or Timbuktu, the mountains sure feel like home – a familiarity similar to heading to my family's farm on the windswept prairies.

They often call me back because, as I am hiking over a pass or walking along a ridge, it reminds me that anything is possible – no matter how tough the climb or how heavy the pack on your back.

WHY WE ARE SO DRAWN TO THE MAGNITUDE AND BEAUTY OF MOUNTAINS

Ian Brown

One morning, the mountains that surround Banff disappeared. A bank of cloud had invaded and obscured them. Suddenly, the town was a floating island, a nowhere. It lasted a few days, on and off, and was more unsettling than you'd think. I like having mountains in the backyard. I've come to rely on their strict edges, their implacable, hard-to-impress presence around the human circle of the town. They remind me of a snooty condo board in an exclusive building that will never truly approve of anyone.

Then the bombs went off in Boston, and terrorists were thwarted from derailing a Via Rail train. The Tsarnaev brothers' next stop, we are told, was Manhattan – no less than Times Square. Mountainous events that captured the obsessive attention of the world.

Details are everything. But then the news eats us alive – instead of controlling the furious pace of the present with our screens and our tweets and our multiple technologies, it controls us. We wolf down all the information we can see and end up stuffed with exhausted despair.

As the news flooded in, I kept stepping outside and looking up at the peaks. Every time I did, I felt better.

Human beings have always been drawn to mountains – to climb them, name them, frame them, mine them, "conquer" them. And I'm not the only one who spends a lot of time looking up at them: five million tourists come to Banff every year, and they all take the same pictures.

I've been trying to figure out why.

From the balcony of my northeast-facing room at the Banff Centre, I can see four mountains: Norquay (home to the first rope ski tow in the Rockies, in 1938), Brewster, Cascade and Rundle.

Cascade is the queen, named for the skinny waterfall that hypnotizes drivers as they flow into Banff on the Trans-Canada Highway from the east. Cascade is the blowsy turret that anchors the end of Banff Avenue, the town's main street. A wide band of snow around its midsection funnels down into four gullies, and looks very much like a garter belt. At 2998 metres, she's a big girl, Cascade, and sexy.

I prefer Rundle, 50 metres lower but more brooding and dramatic, more like a teenager. The southern face of Rundle is a continuous plate that tilts up out of the earth, then drops away on the other side – a 12.5-kilometre wedge between Banff and the town of Canmore, a thrust smeared across the sky. It embodies the contradiction of the mountains: their welcoming intimacy (the gradual slope you can walk up) versus their danger (aiieeeeeeeee!).

Overall, Rundle looks like a massive shoulder leaning into whatever's coming. The cliffs of its peak, however, appear so private and intimate that they can take your breath away. It seems impossible something so close is nine hours distant on foot.

You've probably seen it. Rundle is the most photographed and painted peak in the Rockies. "Mount Rundle is my bread-and-butter mountain," artist Walter Phillips once acknowledged. He was an Englishman who came to teach at the Banff School of Fine Arts in 1940 and stayed for 20 years before he went blind and died three years later. "I never tire of painting it, for it is never the same."

There are entire subgenres of writing and painting dedicated to describing the permanent changeability of mountains and why we long to look at them. But no one has ever nailed the experience once and for all.

Some writers don't even try. Farley Mowat grew up on the Prairies and hated the shadowy, enclosing Rockies from the moment he first saw them as a teenager. He preferred an open landscape, the way others seek the ocean or a beach. A.Y. Jackson never got the hang of painting mountains and admitted as much (he blamed the mountains). Writer Marni Jackson, on the other hand, once described the sight of the Rockies as "a strong signature across the bottom of the sky," and has been using the mountains for inspiration, on and off, for 40 years. Onlookers project onto the Rockies what they need to see.

Not long ago at breakfast, I ran into Kevin Drew, co-founder of the band Broken Social Scene. He had been at the Banff Centre from Toronto for ten days and had written and recorded 14 songs, which seemed like a lot. He was wearing glasses, a blue toque, his usual beard and a large parka that was itself of mountainous loft.

"Do you like the mountains?" I asked.

He said he loved them. "I like being surrounded by the size of them. And I like that you have to be who you are and where you are around the mountains. You can't be anything else. They're demanding."

"Demanding?"

"Because they can be like your elders. They can say, like, 'What were you thinking those last few months? We gave you everything and you come back like this? Get your shit together.' You know?"

Mount Rundle was named for Rev. Robert Rundle, a romantic Wesleyan Methodist missionary from Cornwall, England. In 1840, at the age of 29, he took up an open offer from Hudson's Bay Company Governor George Simpson of transportation, room, board, an interpreter and £50 a year to any clergyman willing to tend the souls of Natives in western North America.

After a 26-day boat journey from Liverpool to New York, and a further three-day trip to Montreal, Rundle set out on April 29, 1840, in a Hudson's Bay canoe – for

Edmonton. He arrived in October, eager to make his way to the Rocky Mountains, which seemed to hold a supernatural allure for him. Some historians claim that he was the first Protestant minister to make it west of Winnipeg.

Judging from sketches, he looked exactly like Charlton Heston in *The Ten Commandments* after Moses receives the tablets from Jehovah – slightly mad, but keen. Finally, in February of the following year, Rundle left Edmonton on the seven-day journey (his first) to Rocky Mountain House and the foothills. He was wearing lamb's wool hose, woolen drawers, lined trousers, leggings, gaiters, a flannel shirt, a waistcoat, a coat, a pilot coat, a shawl, moccasins and a sealskin cap, and was further wrapped in a buffalo robe in his dogsled. Layering, it turns out, has been around a long time.

Rundle's moods swung wildly. He missed England. He suffered from migraines and nosebleeds and thought that the sled driver mistreated the dogs. He also found that roasted beaver tasted like pork (delicious) and that travelling at night prevented snow blindness. By the end of the month, his longed-for mountains were still disappointingly obscure. "How uncertain is everything here below," he wrote in his journal, adding that "much depends on the state of the atmosphere."

In the meantime, he encountered a party of much-feared Blackfoot Indians. "I felt the insignificance of my stature in comparison to these tall sons of the plain," he wrote. But Rundle had a way with Natives: the Blackfoot invited him to their camp. He spent more time with the friendlier Stoney Indians, who believed that he had descended to earth from heaven, folded up in a piece of paper.

April had come around before Rundle recorded having a good look at the mountain peaks, albeit from a distance. "The sight seemed too grand and too glorious for reality," he noted. He thought the view was a preview of what he would see in heaven. He finally breached the front ranges and reached what is now Banff, "quite amongst the mountains," in 1847 – "a time never to be forgotten." To honour the occasion, he conducted services by moonlight in Cree. I wish I'd seen that.

On his way back to Edmonton, he fell off his horse (something he did with regularity) and broke a wrist so badly that the arm was nearly useless, forcing a trip back to England at the age of 39.

He never returned. But Rundle's good reputation with local tribes persisted, so much so that when James Hector, the lead geologist and surgeon of the Palliser Expedition, which was surveying routes for the Canadian Pacific Railway, passed through the area in 1858, the Stoneys were still singing hymns and praying. Hector named Mount Rundle for the earnest reverend. The mountain proceeded to make its next mark in Canadian history by blocking the way of the oncoming railway.

The CPR had hired Major A.B. Rogers, an American, to find a route through the Rockies. (Rogers Pass, the site of some of the best skiing and worst avalanches in Canada, is named for him.) He was an impatient, irascible ass – his mustache was so long and white and thick that it looked as though two streams of smoke were billowing from his infuriated nostrils – who proposed getting around Rundle by running the railway through its much smaller neighbour, Sleeping Buffalo Mountain, via a 275-metre tunnel. CPR president William Cornelius Van Horne was outraged at the projected delay and cost, so the idea was dropped. But the mountain is still called Tunnel, except by the Blackfoot and other tribes, who stick with Sleeping Buffalo – what it looks like if approached from the west.

At least four geological thrusts come to a head in the area, and one of the seismic consequences is the Banff hot springs. Native tribes considered the springs sacred, given their power to heal the wounded, but also as a sign that there was a lot of disruptive mojo in the Bow Valley, both good energy and bad. "They selected Buffalo Mountain as the place where the spirits gather," a Blackfoot Elder named Tom Crane Bear told me one afternoon. We were sitting at a table overlooking the peaks to the west of town, Sulphur and Bourgeau and beyond.

"But why do that on a mountain at all?" I asked.

"Well," Elder Tom said, "you believe in heaven? Everyone believes in some form of heaven. The higher you get, you won't have a problem getting the rest of the way up."

"Why don't Natives climb mountains, then, the way other people do?"

He looked at me. He spoke with long pauses, the way Native Elders sometimes do. "Well, we don't have the equipment, number one. But what's the use of climbing the mountain? There's nothing up there. So we don't climb the mountains."

Others do. Mountains emit a siren call to challengers: their steepness and remoteness, their disdain for human access, seem to offend our pipsqueak egos. This past ski season, one of the must-do tricks for skilled teenage hot-doggers was to ski an exceptionally steep run at Kicking Horse Mountain Resort in Golden, just across the BC border, while naked – or, failing that, to ski it nonstop while placing a cellphone call to your mom halfway down.

The climber who made the official first ascent of Rundle in 1888, J.J. McArthur, made no fewer than 160 such ascents from 1887 to 1893. The CPR's Van Horne (who was, among other things, a painter) understood the appeal from the start: to attract paying passengers to his new railway (and later to his luxury châteaus), he touted "the challenge of the mountains" and their "1,100 unclimbed peaks."

After an American climber fell to his death attempting a first ascent of Mount Lefroy near Lake Louise, the CPR hired Swiss guides Eduard Feuz Sr. and Christian Häsler to haul wealthy tourists safely upward. From 1899 to 1954, the 25 Swiss guides employed by the CPR never suffered a casualty. Conrad Kain, the famed Austrian guide, made 60 virgin ascents (often falling back at the last moment to let his paying client take the glory), and then wrote a memoir, *Where the Clouds Can Go*, in which he laid out his essential rules for guides. Number one was *Never show fear*. Number four was *Lie when necessary*.

Feuz and Häsler begat the likes of Norwegian Erling Strom, North America's first professional ski instructor, who helped to persuade the railway to build Assiniboine Lodge, the backcountry's first (still operating); Strom begat Bruno Engler, the mountaineering filmmaker, and Hans Gmoser, inventor of heli-skiing. (The two guided Pierre Trudeau into the Bugaboos in the early 1970s.)

Gmoser's doctor, Smitty Gardner, asked him to take his son, Don, into the mountains. Don Gardner, in the company of Banff-based writer and explorer Chic Scott and others, made the first Great Divide ski traverse across a mass of icefields from Jasper to Lake Louise, to cite just one of their remarkable exploits. Gardner had a thing for Rundle, too: he hiked up its Banff edge, traversed the long ridge and descended into Canmore, in winter.

The history of the Rockies is knotted up like this, incestuous and interconnected, local history and local memory made bigger by the mountains that people from around the world cannot help but explore, traverse, climb up, ski down, hike or just adore.

The other day in a house next to the Bow River, I heard Chic Scott conduct a fireside chat with Ralphine Locke, an octogenarian who as a child knew many of the pioneers who settled Banff. She remembered the yellow cars that collected the first tourists from the train station on Victoria Day weekend. (In those days, the Banff Springs Hotel shut down for winter.) "That's how you knew it was spring." The house was packed with locals hanging on Ralphine's every word – their living connection to the early history of their town.

Mountains have this macro-scoping effect. The weather can shift and turn circumstances deadly on ten minutes' notice, even on a mountain highway: you have to pay attention and plan for a range of eventualities. The reward for such deliberateness is both a sense of being able to handle yourself and resignation in the face of inevitable change and random chance. When Eduard Feuz was helped up to the high country for a last visit before he died in 1944, he stood and called out goodbye to each of the surrounding peaks. I can only imagine how devastated he must have been, knowing that he would never return to that clean, pure, practical place.

The outside world breaks through the protective ring of the mountains regardless. From Banff, via Twitter and cable and website, last week's bombings in Boston were clearly horrific but somehow seemed to lack the conviction of international terrorism. (Deaths notwithstanding, the maiming they caused may be the most persistent legacy of the Tsarnaev brothers, their most potent symbol.) Everyone in Banff seemed to have watched the footage, but – as was not the case in cities in the East – no one mentioned it unless I brought up the subject. Maybe it was because Boston is a long way from Banff. Or maybe the mountains make you private.

One evening while I was asking people why mountains mattered, I had dinner with Charles Noble, a well-known western poet, and Dave Eso, an emerging one. Mr. Eso is in his 30s and was taking part in a workshop for experimental spoken-word poets at the Banff Centre. He admired the work of Mr. Noble, who is in his 60s and is a part-time Banff resident, and had invited him to dinner at the centre. The poets in the seminar were lively types, working on monologues and performance pieces and songs about such subjects as fear and drunken dates and what it means to say "I love you," especially prematurely.

Charles and Dave are intimidating conversationalists. They talked about Marx and Heidegger. They talked about forms of rhetoric, about how sometimes experimental poets want to avoid "intentionality" or any appearance that they are doing anything so dorky as actually "writing" a "poem," because that way they might attain a less artificial authorial stance and hence deeper feeling. Poetry is a brainy pastime, especially these days.

Suddenly, I realized that experimental poets and people who like to look up at mountains are doing the same thing, just in opposite directions: the poets try to take something abstract, like an idea, and make it concrete, whereas admirers of mountains try to take something huge made of rock and ice and snow and turn it into an abstraction they can carry around in their minds, a mental key chain from a place that is hard to get to but gorgeous to think about.

I suppose what the mountains seduce us with, in the end, is the promise of solitude – the chance to get where hardly anyone gets to go, up high, to the top, alone. Among the high peaks, the promise whispers, you will finally have a chance to think for yourself, to be an individual, beholden to no one, and nothing, and no event – a ridiculous fantasy that has been criticized by Freudians and philosophers as the irresponsible selfishness of thrill-seekers and introverts and narcissists.

In 1972, in a paper entitled "Psychopathology in Alpinism" in the *Canadian Alpine Journal*, a group of researchers concluded that the "mean personality type" of alpinists displayed "schizothymic features and a tendency to avoid contact with other persons." As if that were a bad thing.

But mountains also make you humble. They remind us how much we need to experience beauty, and how rarely we do; of how crushing it can be not to get where you always longed to go, and how that disappointment can make you deeper. They remind us how carelessly we surrender our privacy and our solitude to the phone, the screen and the keyboard, and to others.

I know Elder Tom and the Blackfoot say there is nothing at the top of the mountain, but that presumes nothing has no value. Because this is the other thing: when I step out on my tiny balcony to see those peaks, I often remember poet Mary Oliver's questioning of "the empty spaces / of the wilderness":

> For something is there,
> something is there when nothing is there but itself,
> that is not there when anything else is.

"Formless, yet palpable," as she put it, "Very shining, very delicate. / Very rare." Something you need to believe still exists when you return to the flat, hot, terrified city.

THE COLOUR OF JANUARY

Jocey Asnong

The sky tonight is the particular shade of periwinkle blue that comes only once a year in the Bow Valley. The colour of early twilight in winter looks more like lavender than blue against the brilliant white of the snow-covered Fairholme Range outside of Banff as I follow the curve of the Trans-Canada Highway toward Canmore. It cannot be mixed on my palette, although I have tried for many years. It is the blue of deep cold and suspended ice crystals as the last light of the day pauses briefly on these limestone and shale spires.

When I first moved to this valley at the end of a winter almost two decades ago, I drowned.

This was not unexpected. In my childhood, I had been given a vision of my death during a feverish dream. As I lay sleeping in a tangle of flannel snowflake sheets and my favourite polka dot pajamas, I dreamed that I was drowning in a lake made of turquoise and clay. I grew up by the Great Lakes, but this lake from my nocturnal imagination was unlike anything I had ever experienced or could understand. I gasped for air but instead gulped chalky mouthfuls of opaque water, slowly submerging underwater. I carried the unsettling dream with me into adulthood, occasionally attempting to paint the vivid details of this extraordinary lake onto canvas. I could never capture the depth of colours or understand the context of my departure. Was it symbolic or spiritual, or an intuitive warning to just stay away from water? Along with my pencil crayons and portfolio, I carried this fear of drowning with me when I left my childhood behind to attend art college. I never expected that a chance opportunity to work in the Rockies one summer for tuition would bring me face to face with the meaning of my childhood dream.

As the winter snows receded that June, my new home among the mountains began to seduce me. This landscape is not my original home. I had to come here by leaving everything and everyone I knew behind. I yearned for vertical horizon lines without ever having seen a mountain. I ached for ice and rock as though some part of my soul had been ripped from me at birth. How can you miss something so intimately without ever knowing it personally?

The glacier-fed lake nestled in the Valley of the Ten Peaks begins to thaw and fills with the cerulean blues of my childhood dream; a blue so intense that it refracts all light as it licks along the shore, looking for me.

I recognize this lake.

I stand on the remnants of moraine and mountain and take my final breaths as colour and lake engulf me.

I sink through layers of turquoise and rock flour fills my lungs. I cannot breathe. I am suspended between two different lives. This is the moment when the person I was no longer exists. But I discover I can breathe underwater, I am home.

Everyone here has a similar story.

Before and after.

Death and birth.

Over the oranges and ambers of summer campfires, we share with each other that moment when the person we once were ended abruptly. We will never go back to the places of our birth and childhood homes.

We are the mutant gene.

The windblown seed.

We are the break in pattern.

I follow paths through the high alpine and reach for the frozen places, imagining an ice age shaping my backyard. The colour of ice is a trick of the light, and I reach for tubes of blue and green instead of white. How can so much colour exist in one single crevasse?

My drawing begins to change. The mountains are demanding and relentless models. I make up personalities to match their magnificent presence on my page. The Valley of Ten becomes a complex set of friendships, loyalties and betrayals. I sketch in the shoulders of alpha leader Mount Temple. Babel takes shape on paper as the neighbourhood gossip. My pencil traces Fay's profile and glacial cloak and I identify with her as the shy one with a secret. Tonsa and Tuzo are long-lost soulmates locked in a splash of watercolour. My sketchbook fills with caricatures and musings and the secret lives of mountains.

As the clouds drop and mark the change between the seasons, I drift down to the valley bottom, following the curve of the Bow River. I learn a new language of colours in this new season.

The cadmium yellow of the turning of the larches.

The lavender greys of the first snowfall.

The indigo blues of a midnight sky over a hushed ski hill in March.

The cobalt blues of snow shadows.

The pea greens of flat light in a blizzard.

The amber golds of the first rays of spring sunlight warming the day lodge.

The sunset pinks of a snow-reflected sunburn.

I trace contour lines and gestures down black diamond ridges and snow bowls. My fear of failing is replaced with the fear of falling, a much easier demon to wrestle with. The treeline lives permanently below me and the high alpine becomes my new canvas. I carve deeply into fresh snow, shaping sculptures and rhythms into the landscape. Winter here is endless and there is no lack of empty white for me to leave my mark.

The headwaters of the Bow River roar back to life as spring returns, and I leave the valley I love and drift north to Jasper. I convince myself that I am looking for a community instead of a tourist trap, a place to call home that isn't staff accommodation.

Perhaps I believe that all valleys are created equal.

I am wrong.

I pour words and poetry onto page, documenting the abrupt changes in my surroundings. The mountains here resemble men's faces and women's hips. They are foreign in a way that I did not expect. I discover that I cannot draw here. This valley is far too wide, with a scar of steel running straight through its heart. Why did I start listening to the voice in my head instead of trusting my heart? How did I take such a misguided detour from the valley I have always loved?

Many of us try to cut our umbilical cord to this landscape. Perhaps this is the season of our adolescence. We have all made sacrifices to live here, and at some point we fall back into the dangerous habit of measuring our lives by the things we don't have and the sad little numbers in our bank accounts. Our faces are flushed with the scarlet reds of frustration as we haul our burden of wish lists and regrets around.

Many leave for the promise of more.

My absence from the Bow Valley stands out from my memories as the charred blacks and charcoals after a forest fire. My drawing and stories are not just interrupted by this change of scenery; they are catastrophically derailed. My paints crack from lack of use. Instead of returning, I drift even farther north, toward the Arctic Circle. I abandon everything. I crack from lack of use.

Some of us return.

The valley forgives us for our foolishness.

We rebuild. We heal.

We stop measuring what we don't have.

I replace my abandoned acrylics with something more forgiving. I mix gouache and water, starting over.

My appreciation runs deeper now, and my colour choices reflect my shift in attitude and acceptance. I reach for another medium that can express the subtle layers of love and loss that are a part of living here. I smudge chalk across black, building on what I have learned.

The stories that I carry now begin to take shape in my studio. I decorate the walls of my art cave and home in Canmore with this newfound narrative. I create imaginary worlds with colour and lines, yet each illustration is a celebration of this sense of place. To be at home and present in this fierce landscape takes just as long and as much practice as to feel at home within your own skin.

Then spring arrives in chaos. The only colours that exist now are the mud browns of Cougar Creek and the silt greys of the Bow River as they gorge across my mountain town, erasing subdivisions and homes in moments. We are reminded that our valley has an ancient and forgotten role as floodplain for an alluvial fan.

And that we are fragile.

We watch the debris of our identities and houses float across prairies to distant oceans, the show-home beiges of our lives are immediately exposed. The sound of rain now triggers nightmares. I am reminded again of the relationship between water and rock. The landscape is fluid here and the mountains have a forward momentum that we collectively forgot has always been out of our control.

We pause to consider that faith can move mountains, and so can rain.

The summer arrives in an unusual celebration of greens and emeralds while we excavate the summits of mountains out of the homes and roadways scattered along the valley bottom.

To live here is to imagine a life lived in harmony with the elements. We adjust our eagle wings and soar on thermals across the peaks and through the gaps, hoping that we don't collide with reality. We congratulate each other over the organic produce bins at the local summer market for last winter's epic powder day or for bagging our first 11,000-foot ascent. We are a like-minded army of multicoloured puffy down jackets mortgaged up to the pompom tops on our ski hats.

To live here for several seasons is to know that this valley will eventually peel all our layers of down and Gore-Tex off and strip us bare to our true authentic messy selves.

Why we are here.

What we ran away from.

Who we really are.

The valley slumbers under blankets of snow this quiet January evening as I drive this familiar road home. I have lived here for almost two decades now, and although I still cannot capture the colour of this January twilight before it deepens to purple, I have managed to find my place in this valley. I think fondly of that young art student I once was, risking everything and redefining her future to move to the Rockies. While I wasn't looking, my time in the mountains has completed the training I left behind so many years ago. I am an illustrator.

WRITTEN IN MY NAME

Joleen Brewster Niehaus

I was born in Banff, Alberta, a small town that lies in the middle of the Bow Valley, surrounded by the beautiful Canadian Rockies. I was born into the Brewster family, where hard work was done without question. On March 17, 1886, John Brewster arrived in Banff. Shortly after, he established a local dairy farm that supplied the Banff Springs Hotel and the citizens of Banff with dairy products. His two eldest sons, William and Jim Brewster, worked in the dairy farm, and at the age of 12 and 13 were given the opportunity to guide guests from the Banff Springs Hotel on a local fishing expedition. This was the beginning of Brewster Mountain Pack Trains.

The relationship with the Banff Springs flourished, and the Brewsters were given the opportunity to transport the guests from the Canadian Pacific Rail to the Banff Springs Hotel on horse-drawn tallyho. This was the start of the Brewster Transfer Company, which was sold to Greyhound in 1965. The winter pasturing ground for the dairy cattle was at the base of Mount Yamnuska; this became the Kananaskis Guest Ranch. The ranch was run by Missy, William Brewster's wife, and his son Claude Bagley Brewster, who was my great-grandfather. Claude was instrumental in bringing Indian Days to Banff and for starting the Sulphur Mountain Gondola.

Fourth-generation Claude (Bud) Brewster, my "grampy," was a big influence in my life; I was lucky enough to develop a strong relationship with him. Being a sixth-generation Brewster has allowed me to have unique opportunities and experiences, but it has also burdened me with tremendous pressure and stress that most teenagers my age don't experience. These opportunities and this pressure have changed the way I see Banff and the Bow Valley.

My grandfather Bud was a strong-willed man with many dreams and aspirations. Through hard work and determination he attained many of his goals throughout his lifetime. Today, my family and I strive to continue the legacy that Bud laid out. Bud Brewster was born in Canada and grew up at the Kananaskis Guest Ranch in the shadow of Mount Yamnuska. Though he vowed never to marry, in 1959 he got hitched to Annette, a young prairie girl who at the time was working at Lake O'Hara. Bud and Annette took the reigns of Brewster's pack trains, which outfitted the trail riders of the Canadian Rockies, and the skyline hikers, a commercial guiding operation in the mountains. With the help of his three daughters and their husbands, he successfully built Brewster MountView Barbecue, Brewster Mountain Lodge and the Brewster Kananaskis Golf Resort.

My grandfather was never an affectionate man. He had great success in business, and maybe because that was his focus he didn't show his fondness for his grandchildren often. When he did, he would do it by patting us on the head or trying to trip us with his walking cane. Although he didn't smother us with hugs and kisses, my family all knew that was his way of showing that he truly loved us. It didn't matter to my grandfather if you were a girl, you could be tougher than any cowboy he knew if you wanted to. When I first got bucked off my horse, I was startled and I began to cry. My grandfather picked me up off the dirt, dusted my jeans off and told me not to cry, because I needed to get back in the saddle and show my horse that I was tougher than him.

I never saw my grandfather without a lit cigarette in one hand and a glass of rye in the other. He used to drive around Banff in his old Chevy pickup truck, barely tall enough to see out the window, drifting around every gravel-coated turn he could find. My grandfather led a hard life, and his hard work led to great success, which later led to health troubles. True to character, he refused to listen to his doctors and his wife. He kept drinking and smoking, living every day to the fullest.

Bud Brewster rode his last horse out on Banff's Buffalo Street on February 10, 2012. We celebrated his life with an Irish wake at MountView Barbecue, which was his second home. To honour his memory, my sister and I took a sip of his favourite whiskey and shed a tear or two. I will always remember Bud as a rugged cowboy, carpenter, businessman, entrepreneur, but most importantly my grandfather, who taught me how important it is never to give up on your dreams, no matter how many obstacles stand in the way. My family and I owe everything to my grandfather because he built the Brewster name into what it is today. I cannot imagine what my family would be like if Bud hadn't pursued his dreams and ambitions.

Some aspects of growing up in Banff were pretty normal, like going to school and making good friends. Some aspects were not. Since the age of five months old, I have spent every summer and many winters at my family's backcountry lodge. Brewster Shadow Lake Lodge is approximately 14 kilometres into the mountains, high above the Bow Valley. My parents took over the Canadian Pacific Railway cabin there in 1985. After fighting a decade-long fight with Parks Canada, they managed to build 15 more cabins with the help of family and friends. My parents got us deep into the backcountry many different ways: they wrapped us in sleeping bags and shoved us onto a back of a skidoo, or balanced us on the horn of my father's horse. I remember being little, barely tall enough to see over the kitchen countertops at Shadow Lake, and watching my mother cook. To me it looked so fun, cutting all the vegetables, stirring all the soups, baking all the bread. I didn't realize how much work it all was. I would always "help" my dad by following him around the lodge on his many chores. I always thought I was a big help, when in reality I was probably more of a nuisance.

As soon as my sister and I were old enough, our parents put us to work. When I was 6 years old, I started in the dish pit like all new employees; then I got to bake cookies, although I think I ate more cookie dough than I actually baked. By the age of 10 I had started to help my father on pack day. This involved getting up at the crack of dawn in Banff, packing the groceries and clean sheets, saddling our nine horses and then trailing them up the 14-kilometre trail to Shadow Lake. Then we'd collect the dirty laundry and garbage and ride the trail back home. I would frequently help my father pull ropes while we "threw the diamond hitch," which is the knot used for securing loads to the pack horses. We would then tie the horses into the pack string, which was led by my father, and set off. My favourite part was keeping my father company during the 28-kilometre round trip. There was always lots of singing and storytelling. When I reached the age of 13, I started working as a full-time cabin girl. I was put on the schedule, which meant I had to mountain bike in to Shadow Lake and work for a week straight along with our co-workers that season. My parents relied on my sister and I to pick up the slack, calling us when the others failed to show up for work, or when they were too strung out themselves.

I learned from an early age that the statement "I don't know" or "I can't do it" was not a valid answer to a question in my family. I feel like I have always had more responsibility than other people my age. I learned to take responsibility because the slightest slip-up could result in the customers leaving with a negative impression of my family's business.

As we grew up, my older sister wouldn't let me act like a dumb, rebellious teenager, because she knew it wouldn't help me. Now my sister is going to college, and

I have to make my own hard decisions about what I'm going to do when I get older. I am very proud and thankful for the things I get to do. I feel pressure because I am a part of two special family businesses that have such a rich history. I am the sixth generation of Brewsters in the Canadian Rockies, and I feel like I need to keep the family name and businesses going. I know if I don't participate when I get older that I am going to feel incredibly guilty. I do not want to let my parents or sister down, and I want to live up to the values of hard work and pride in our family history that both my parents have. Some days I can't see myself in my parents' shoes, but, then again, I can't imagine selling our family businesses and watching some random strangers run them.

I often ask myself the question: Do I want to carry on with my family business, or do I want to start and do something else in my life? When I think about the pros and cons to both sides, I can't imagine leaving Banff, where I have such deep roots. When I think of my life growing up in Banff, I realize that I want my future children to have the same experiences I have. I can imagine taking over the family businesses when I'm ready, but that definitely won't be easy. I know I'll have my sister by my side throughout the whole thing. And I always know that my grampy will be watching over me and also keeping an eye on his business from up there.

Some people ask me what it's like being a Brewster and growing up in a family business. Most of the time I am lost for words, because being a Brewster is more than just a family business, it's a way of life. I guess it's written in my name.

EXSHAW

THE BEST-KEPT SECRET

Ruth Oltmann

The distinctive flat face of Mount Laurie (Îyâmnathka), commonly called Mount Yamnuska, lies north of the Bow River and is often the first mountain seen when travelling west from the city of Calgary. Seven kilometres west of this mountain lies the small hamlet of Exshaw, on Highway 1A. It was here in 1906 that a plant to manufacture cement was established by the Western Canada Cement & Coal Company, and workers were recruited from all over Canada and Europe. Logging and limestone extraction had taken place in the area for several years, but it was this company's work that resulted in the small community of Exshaw being established. Today, it consists of less than 400 people who feel it is the best-kept secret in the Bow Valley. The hamlet's slogan, "Heart of the Valley," stems from Heart Mountain on the south side of the Bow River, which can be seen from everywhere in the hamlet.

The history of the hamlet, *Exshaw: Heart of the Valley,* was published in 2005 and is a large volume, spearheaded and written by Dene Cooper and Rob Alexander, with contributions from others such as myself. The many intriguing stories of the early explorers who passed through the area, combined with descriptions of life in Exshaw over the years, gives a sense of place in the history of the Bow Valley. Most people do not know that at one time Exshaw was part of Rocky Mountains Park (now Banff National Park). From 1916 to 1930, the park encompassed a large area extending south into the Kananaskis Valley and north into what is now the forest reserve, and thus included Exshaw. However, in 1930, the national park changed its boundary and Exshaw and the Kananaskis Valley were no longer in the park.

One of the unique historical aspects of the hamlet is the five "catalogue" houses still in use today that were purchased through the Eaton's catalogue after the Second World War. The buildings came in sections and were erected by the owners with the help of their friends. A postwar form of prefabricated housing. Even in the early years there was a strong bond among the residents, as men were often seen on their days off walking around the hamlet with shovels and tools in hand, checking to see who they could help with home construction projects. While the men worked at construction, the women, who were wonderful cooks, would provide meals. Today, this sense of community is still prevalent.

In that vein, in September 2015, I organized a community event I called Exshaw Mountain Day, where anyone in the community was invited to register and hike up the mountain, stopping at two stations along the flagged route to the summit cairn. Those who reached the top received a prize on their return. It was a huge success, with 52 adults and children (dogs were not counted) registered, and a lot of fun, especially with families of young children, and was followed by a barbeque. Everyone is keen to make it an annual event.

Most people think of Exshaw as the home of rock industry workers, but it is far more than that. The inhabitants come from a wide variety of occupations, such as schoolteachers; Kananaskis Country employees; LafargeHolcim (cement), Graymont (lime) and Baymag (magnesium) employees; plus plumbers, carpenters, nurses, river guides, mountain guides, massage therapists, hairdressers, writers and more.

As a new Kananaskis Country government employee, I came to the hamlet in 1981 because it was the closest place to Kananaskis and the Barrier Lake Visitor Centre where I could find a place to rent. Subsequently, I bought property, and I stayed when I retired because I had put down roots. I love my home with its wonderful mountain views, and the community suits me. I never did consider Canmore.

When the Heart Mountain Go-Getters was raised from cooling ashes, I became involved. It is now an active seniors group that meets twice a month for socials, bowling, tours and various other projects and activities. The annual Christmas potluck party is a highlight of the year. Many of the seniors have known each other for 30 or more years, and some of the men who have grown up in Exshaw can be very entertaining when recounting stories of their childhood escapades. A number of the seniors who have chosen to retire in the hamlet have also become involved in these activities.

The hamlet isn't just attractive to seniors, it is also very attractive to young families, who have become an integral part of the community and consider it a wonderful place to raise children. The Sports Day, hosted by the Legion for the children in the early summer, is very popular, with a parade of fire trucks and 20 or more children on bicycles, followed by sports events and a barbeque. The two playgrounds in the hamlet are popular with young children.

The Exshaw Legion, originally part of the old town before the 1973 plant expansion, has been part of the community since the Second World War and sponsors a number of events throughout the year, such as poker games, a meat draw, bingo, dances with bands, and special dinners. This little hamlet may be the only place where every child under 12 receives a Christmas present from Santa, during the Legion's children's Christmas party. During Seniors Week in June, the Legion has been hosting a luncheon for local and former Exshaw seniors.

The Exshaw Community Association is also very active. Every adult in the community is considered a member. The executive meets on a monthly basis to discuss information received from the municipal district, plans for trails, events, industry concerns, general upkeep of the children's parks and the hamlet. The ECA is the community liaison for classes and programs, Legion events, community events and community concerns. It is also responsible for everything related to the Community Centre, such as rentals, bills, upkeep and rebuilding, and the campground and ball diamond. An ice rink is a project it is currently working on, as well as the popular gym. Occasionally, there is a fundraising casino.

The Community Centre is owned by the association and houses a gym, a hall and the seniors' facility. The hall is popular for weddings, receptions, meetings and a variety of other events.

There are many keen mountain bikers, hikers, runners and climbers in the community. Mount Fable, as seen when driving north on Windridge Road, is a popular peak to climb in the spring, but there are also mountain biking and hiking trails that appeal to these enthusiasts. Like Canmore, it is a sporting community.

The Exshaw Heritage Society is interested in preserving the historic St. Bernard's Catholic Church building, which was built in 1907 and was in part of the original hamlet. As an interested historian, I became involved from the start. The church building had to be moved in 2014 to make room for the expansion of the Lafarge-Holcim plant. Fortunately, Graymont offered a place on its land for temporary storage of the building. The society is now looking for donated land within the hamlet as a permanent site for the building and is discussing what would be a viable use that would benefit the whole community.

The Municipal District of Bighorn's Heritage Resources Committee covers all the heritage resources in the

MD but also focuses on Exshaw and its historical resources. History is not allowed to fade into obscurity.

KanBow Birders is a birding group made up of Exshaw and Canmore residents. They are particularly active during the spring and the Christmas bird counts and the golden eagle migration count.

Exshaw School covers kindergarten to Grade 8 and has a high percentage of students from the Stoney Reserve, east of Exshaw. Since English is usually a second language for these students, there is a reading program through volunteers for those requiring help. The school Christmas concert is a popular event, with many parents attending. During Seniors Week in June, the Grade 8 students host a Seniors Tea with fancy cakes and entertainment. At the end of the school year, the Grade 8 Farewell program is held for the graduates. Lafarge-Holcim offers various initiatives to the school, working with the children and providing tours of the plant. Earth Day is celebrated, the tennis court at the school has a clean-up day and Baymag works with the children picking litter along Highway 1A.

Graymont provides a Stampede Breakfast for the community during the Calgary Stampede and at the same time offers tours of its lime plant and its quarry on Grotto Mountain.

LafargeHolcim has been involved in several community initiatives over the years and more recently established the Lafarge Education Endowment Fund scholarship, which awards $5,000 grants to MD of Bighorn students pursuing post-secondary education. The Community Liaison Committee, made up of Exshaw,

Lac des Arcs and Harvie Heights residents, meets to discuss concerns and initiatives.

Downtown Exshaw, if you can call it that, consists of the Heart Mountain Store, with gas pumps and a café; the post office; and the Municipal District of Bighorn offices. The Bighorn Library is housed in the basement of the MD building. The fire hall is a short distance from the store. The men and women who volunteer their services in firefighting and rescue missions take care of the fire trucks and have regular practice sessions.

The Bighorn Library goes back to 1977, when the Exshaw Community Library was formed. Originally it was in the Exshaw School but was moved around several times. For awhile it was in the former credit union building (that business had closed after a holdup), and for awhile it was in the 1907 St. Bernard's Catholic Church building. It finally came to rest in the basement of the Municipal District when the MD acquired a building from the 1988 Olympics. This allowed the library to expand, and it soon joined the Marigold Library System. It also joined the digital age, acquiring computers hooked into the Internet. The children's story and craft times have continued over the years and are very popular. One can also order books through a number of systems, not just the Marigold. Occasionally, when I have become interested in an obscure subject, I have received books from universities. The library is a focal point in the hamlet for all ages, and the friendly, helpful staff are indispensable to the sense of place in the community.

In the early days of the hamlet, prior to the 1973 Lafarge plant expansion, the downtown and most of the houses were on the west side of Exshaw Creek and the hamlet was much larger, with a hotel, two churches, a store, a skating rink and a cenotaph, as well as many homes. During those early days, a dairy operated on the east side of the creek in what is now referred to as Knowlerville (named after an original owner). One of the houses in that area is partly constructed of logs and dates back to 1907, although the logs have not been visible for many years due to various types of siding.

An industrial park on Diamond Drive is the home of several businesses, with the ball diamond and campground located at the east end of the drive.

Exshaw is a hamlet where people have come together and formed a friendly, caring community; while it is usually ignored by the towns of Canmore and Banff, its own residents know their sense of place. This caring atmosphere was particularly evident during the big flood of 2013, when Exshaw Creek, Jura Creek and Grotto Creek overflowed and created extensive damage through massive amounts of rock and water. The community pulled together and helped those in need and showered each other with kindness and caring. Exshaw School hosted evacuees and was a friendly meeting place for those who were hurting emotionally. Food and Red Cross beds and blankets had to be flown into the isolated hamlet for several days. Lafarge came to the rescue of the fire hall, which was about to be washed down the creek, by providing large rocks to shore up the building. Other big rocks provided by Lafarge helped protect the hamlet and other places throughout the province from the devastation.

This quiet hamlet offers a special way of life and that ever-looked-for sense of place for people interested in getting off the beaten path and being part of a caring community, and provides activities they can become involved in if they wish. It is one of those rare places where if you don't show up for an event you were to be attending, someone will go and find you, and if they have a key to your house, they will get in and look for you or, at least, look in your Day-timer to see where you may be. Rescue is just around the corner, and if you are ill or injured, the traditional Canadian casserole may arrive at your door.

Exshaw really is the best-kept secret in the Bow Valley!

DOWNRIVER

Stephen Legault

When I first landed in the Bow Valley, I did so much closer to the source of the watershed. In the 25 years I've lived here, I've slowly drifted downstream. It feels like the natural order of things, to allow the current of life to take one downriver, away from the source and toward our eventual confluence with all things.

Lake Louise is tucked into an alpine valley off the main stem of the Bow River. It's known around the world as a picture-perfect mountain landscape, and each year more than two million people stand on its shore – if only for a few moments – to take a snapshot or a selfie before hurrying on.

I had no idea where Lake Louise was when I was hired to work there, despite its notoriety.

The phone call came late in the spring. I was finishing my second – and, as it turns out, final – year of college in a natural resource management program in Lindsay, Ontario. I loved nature, wanted to be a "Park Ranger" and had applied to more than 90 provincial and national parks earlier in the spring. I had already had job interviews with the Pinery Provincial Park and St. Lawrence Islands National Park, both in Ontario. There had been no job offers yet.

Something in me yearned for mountains. A few years before, I had considered running away from home and high school and heading to California to live in the Sierra Nevada as John Muir had once done. I had read Muir's *My First Summer in the Sierra*, and considered Ansel Adams my photographic hero, and wanted to see what they had seen and feel what they had felt. The mountains of Western Canada seemed further away in my hormone-stricken teenaged brain than did the high Sierra.

It's unlikely I would have gotten out of the Greater Toronto Area at that age, but it was a fantasy to live somewhere wild and open, and not Ontario. As the end of my second year in college approached, I applied to all of Canada's mountain national parks.

The call was from a man named Mike Kerr. I had interviewed for a position in Banff National Park, and we had discussed the possibility of my working in the Banff townsite, doing a combination of interpretation and graphic design work, neither of which I knew much about. Mike was calling to offer me a summer position, but there was a change of plans. He wanted to know if I would consider working as a full-time park interpreter – about as close as I could come to being a ranger – in Lake Louise. I calmly said yes, I would love to, and then proceeded to call all my friends over for a party.

The next day, I had to go to my school's library to find out where Lake Louise was.

I arrived in Alberta a few weeks later. I was picked up at the airport by Doug Brown, another Park Service employee, and he asked if I wanted to stop and get something to eat. I bought two Subway sandwiches because I had no idea if I would be able to find dinner in Lake Louise.

The summer before, I had lived and worked at a small provincial park in south-central Ontario called Murphys Point. It was tucked away in the hills of the Frontenac Axis, a 40-kilometre-wide neck of Canadian Shield that extended south from Algonquin Provincial Park, across the St. Lawrence Seaway and into upstate New York. Murphys Point was in the middle of nowhere, or at least pretty close. The nearest town was 20 kilometres away, which may as well have been on the moon, because I didn't have a car. I expected Lake Louise to be more of the same and was elated by the prospect.

Provisioned with my sandwiches, we drove out of Calgary and toward the mountains. The anticipation had been building in me for the two weeks since I'd been offered the job. Helpful people had offered insight on what it would be like to see the mountains rising up from the prairie for the first time: exhilarating, magical, life-changing. I had been up since four a.m., so I fell asleep, missing my chance at resplendent glory. I woke as we passed the cement plants in Exshaw.

I soon learned that there *was* food in Lake Louise – though it was very expensive – and much, much more. There were mountains, wild rivers, grizzly bears and hiking trails beyond counting that set my heart on fire. And there was a hotel on the lake. A huge hotel. And a lot of people.

At Murphys Point I'd lived in a modest-sized cabin on a granite hill above tranquil Loon Lake. Each morning I'd woken early and with a cup of tea in hand I'd traipsed down to the lakeshore, watched the nesting pair of loons I named Harold and Maude, and the snapping turtle I'd named Igor, and then pushed the giant 19-foot aluminum Grumman canoe into the water for a quick paddle before heading in to work.

I was horrified to learn that there would be no quiet mornings on this lakeshore, not with the hulking behemoth of the Chateau Lake Louise towering above the emerald waters.

I suppose I should have done some more research before taking the job. This was before the Internet, and it never occurred to me that anybody would let a company, no matter how steeped in Canadian history, do what Canadian Pacific had done on the shore of this iconic lake.

My first summer was pretty much perfect, except for the growing knot of frustration in my belly about the shoddy condition of Canada's flagship national park. In the first week of September, I left Lake Louise – not for the last time – and returned to "Onterrible," where I worked for my college as a consultant on sustainability issues. A friend sent me back issues of the local newspaper; I read Sid Marty's *Men for the Mountains*, and I listened to Blue Rodeo's song "Western Skies" over and over again. I was lonesome and homesick and felt suddenly out of place in the place where I had grown up.

You're not always born or raised in a place you can call home, but you can choose.

As soon as I got my offer letter from Parks Canada, I was back on a plane and bound for the mountains I'd grown to love.

As the seasons rolled by, I grew less and less tolerant of the destruction of the mountain parks, and the erosion of the park experience for the visitor. Instead of coming to see the mountains, and maybe endure a few discomforts in doing so, visitors were shielded from a genuine connection with nature and instead funnelled into the waiting arms of Banff's retailers.

In my frustration, I became an activist. I'd already been agitating for a number of years about consumer waste, our disposable society, climate change (I first got concerned about this in 1989); now my anger was fixed on those who were selling out Canada's most beautiful landscapes to greedy developers. It didn't sit well with Parks Canada to see me on the television or read my name in the newspaper, advocating for less development.

I made a lot of mistakes in doing so. In my youthful enthusiasm, I foolishly used Parks Canada's telephones, computers and fax machines to aid and abet in my agitation. I never spoke ill of my employer while guiding visitors up into the craggy hills, but I didn't pull any punches when I criticized them and their pals in the development community when talking with the media or writing letters to the editor in my off-time.

The writing was on the wall when, at a large gathering of staff with the regional director, I asked the following question: How would Parks Canada meet its mandate for conservation when it was cutting the budgets of the departments that did the conservation work? It was a pretty innocuous question, I thought, but the explosive response of the senior bureaucrat left an echoing silence in the room. A couple of weeks later, I learned that I wouldn't be asked to return to Parks the following summer. I was given a few days to pack my things and leave staff housing. It was the week before Christmas.

I drifted downriver. I came to rest in a small backwater eddy called Harvie Heights, a few kilometres from Canmore, on the border of Banff National Park. It was quiet, many of the homes occupied by weekenders or old-timers from around the valley, and it was perfect. The hamlet was tucked into the trees, edged up against the Fairholme Range and its narrow slot canyons.

Freed of both employment and the constraints that came with it, I was able to turn my attention nearly full-time to activism and writing. This was 20 years ago, and it's been like that ever since.

The best thing about living in Harvie Heights was its proximity to nature. Just a stone's throw from the basement apartment I rented was a network of trails that forked through the lodgepole pine and aspen woods, up along the ridgeline called Sunset that overlooked the standing wave of Mount Rundle and into the mouths of the three narrow limestone canyons.

Nearly every day for the six years I lived in Harvie Heights, I walked those trails. Hundreds of times I crested the ridgeline and looked out across the needle-work of pine tops that swept away toward Banff National Park and up the sheer crest of Rundle. More times than I can count, I walked up through the Kamenka Quarry – something that is strictly forbidden now – and into the mouth of my favourite of the three narrow canyons that slice out of the Fairholme Range. I was there one August day when a flash flood flushed rocks the size of basketballs out the canyon's mouth and down the steps of the 25-metre waterfall. For days afterward, I explored the suddenly unfamiliar defile, marvelling at how an hour of rain could create so much change in a place. I couldn't know at the time how true that would prove to be a decade and a half later.

I might have stayed in Harvie Heights even longer, but the challenges of renting a home finally caught up with me when my first son, Rio, was born. After years of living quietly in this small eddy, my partner and I pushed back into the main stem of the river and paddled hard for another resting place just downstream: Canmore.

These were rougher waters, the waves harder to cut and, for reasons that are no longer important, we decided a few years after buying a condo in Canmore that the Bow Valley no longer felt like home.

My partner at the time, with our 3-year-old son and a second child on the way, shipped oars and left for the West Coast, hoping that whatever troubled us would be settled by distance and difference.

The Bow Valley has many tributaries, but unlike the river that rests at its centre, some of these stems and reaches flow both ways. We took one of these and left the Bow Valley.

So many who come into the Bow find this necessary. It's a hard place to hold an eddy line. It's expensive, and the climate can make settling down difficult. There isn't much summer at all, and during what summer we have, we're crushed with tourists and traffic, and for some that's too much to take. Sometimes the reasons for leaving are deeply personal.

But sometimes we come back.

After five years of living in Victoria, BC, I returned. I'd never really been away; not for very long. During that hiatus on the coast, my new family and I spent a lot of time returning to this watershed. After the self-imposed calamity I wrought on my former relationship settled down, I married a woman as attached to this watershed as I was, and with Rio and Silas we returned. My ex and her new husband also moved back to this place that can have such a powerful hold on the head and the heart, and so together we brought a West Coast sense of extended family back to this landlocked mountain range.

Now I live in Canmore again, and while all of the problems that were here when I left – the busyness, the crush of tourists, the constant battle of development versus conservation – are still here, amplified by the years, the peace of the river's edge we've settled on has a powerful hold.

So many people come to this watershed, set their life's course on the river and look for a place to swing their bow into and live out their lives. Some find quiet waters, and others have to haul their lives out of this rocky flow and search for another place that suits them, or that they suit better.

But for those who drift downriver awhile, scanning the shore for that place called home, the Bow and its deep, wide and awe-inspiring valley can give us exactly what we are searching for: a life lived close to nature, where family and friends and even our visitors share a wild passion for place, community and a life set to the flow of a river.

A SENSE OF MOUNTAIN PLACE

WALLACE STEGNER AND OUR WEST

R.W. Sandford

I would like to begin by explaining how Wallace Stegner has directly affected my life and work. In 2010, I published a book called *Ecology and Wonder in the Canadian Rocky Mountain Parks World Heritage Site*. The contents of this book were founded upon three tenets, the first being that we got the history of the Canadian mountain West backwards, and that it is not what we built here – but what we saved in terms of landscape – that makes us unique as a people.

This notion is based on the fact that 125 years ago we were well on the way to destroying the mountain West.

Then suddenly, in the very midst of fragmenting and developing the mountain West, we recognized there were qualities of place here that meant something more to us than immediate wealth. After discovering what we had, we began to put what we had started to destroy back together again in a semblance of its original pristine form. Not all of us fully realize yet what we have done. What we saved is what makes the West habitable. It is what makes where we live utterly unique. Having such landscapes around us and near us gives us room and makes us unique as a people. The combination of protected landscapes and unique culture is what makes it so worth living here and so attractive as a place to visit.

The second tenet is that if we did this once (that is to say, if we have already reinvented ourselves once), then there is no reason we couldn't do it again – now, if we so wished.

The third tenet of *Ecology and Wonder* was that if, in addition to preserving the landscape, we created a culture worthy of what we protected, what we saved might in the end save us. This, of course, being a reference to continual population growth in the West as a whole and in Canmore and the Bow Valley in particular; to ongoing landscape change in regions surrounding ours; and, of course, to the accelerating effects of climate change that have already begun in our experience of the mountain West in both Canada and the United States.

Although they are unique to this particular region of the Canadian West, and to the Bow Valley specifically, it is accurate to say that each of these ideas had its origins in the writings of Wallace Stegner and a dozen other writers who were – as I was – much inspired by his ideas as they relate to people and place. I am indebted to Wallace Stegner to the extent that each of these ideas emerged directly from the application of his principled approach to first respecting the unique qualities of the West as a place and then establishing an ethical way of living amidst those qualities that does not diminish them.

In order to pay long-overdue homage to Wallace Stegner, I would like to discuss some of the books Stegner wrote and the ideas that he shared that most influenced my view of what it means to live in *our* West; which is to say, the mountain West in Canada. In conclusion, I will return to the three fundamental tenets I explored in *Ecology and Wonder* to see how they fare against the backdrop of what Stegner's life and work have come to mean – and what has happened to the West in both the United States and Canada – in the nearly two decades since his death.

Stegner left us with a lot to read. Over his life he wrote 13 novels, 9 major works of nonfiction, 242 nonfiction articles and 57 short stories in magazines and newspapers.

While I have not always agreed with his observations regarding the influence of outside others on place, I have never ceased to respect his power to give meaning and value to where and how we live in the West. I have also observed that his views, like mine, changed over time as he matured and as the West itself changed.

It is interesting to note that Stegner did not pay much attention to *our* West. As far as I know Stegner only visited the Canadian Rockies once – this garnered from a description of a camping trip he made with his father to Banff National Park, probably in the 1960s, to which Page Stegner made fleeting reference in his own book on rafting down the Grand Canyon. Though, as he observed later in his life, Stegner was probably two inches of rain away from becoming a Canadian before his family's Saskatchewan farm was sunburned out of existence in 1920, we were not part of the West as he defined it in his writing. While Saskatchewan was certainly part of that West, the Alberta Rockies were not, at least not directly. This does not mean, however, that what he wrote about does not pertain here.

Wallace Stegner had a very difficult upbringing. It marked him for the rest of his life. His father despised Wallace's bookishness and was often brutal in his resentment of his son's small physical size and weaknesses. After rains stopped falling and crops started to fail in Saskatchewan in 1915, George Stegner took up gambling and then turned to bootlegging to support his family. Over time, his family appeared to matter to him less and less.

Stegner's father was an archetypical raider, a dreamer who never quit searching for the big strike, the get-rich-quick scheme that would set him free. Sabrina, a character in *All the Little Live Things*, utters a line that would have described Stegner's father: "His was the kind that left eroded gulches" – and that he did. George Stegner eventually abandoned his wife, who later died of cancer. His own life skidded to an unseemly end on June 15, 1939, when he shot and killed a 38-year-old divorcee he had been seeing in the lobby of a sleazy Salt Lake City hotel. After murdering Dorothy LeRoy, the senior Stegner turned the gun on himself and took his own life.

Stegner called the book he wrote about growing up in such a family *The Big Rock Candy Mountain*. The title comes from a line in a Depression-era song written by Harry McClintock that became popular with the hobo class that came into existence as a result of the collapse of the American economy caused by Wall Street malfeasance. (Evidently, some things never change.) Stegner later borrowed from the lyrics of the same song for the title of *Where the Bluebird Sings to the Lemonade Springs*.

After receiving a new typewriter as a present, Stegner began writing *The Big Rock Candy Mountain* over the Christmas holidays in 1937. Initially, it was Stegner's intent to write a book about what he called his "orphaned and symbolic" family. But the plot soon thickened.

The Big Rock Candy Mountain was the first major novel in which Stegner consciously explored the notion of synecdoche. Synecdoche, Stegner later explained to his students, was the combination of opinions, emotions and behaviour that characterized a people in the context of place. Stegner worked hard to have individual characters in his novels be representative of the larger milieu in which they lived.

As one biographer described it, *The Big Rock Candy Mountain* is a history of a family as seen through the eyes of the single surviving son. Stegner described it as a "psychological novel concerned with the intimate effects of character on character and generation on generation."

Because it is so unflinchingly personal, some of you may find *The Big Rock Candy Mountain* a painful book to read. Certainly I did. Stegner attempts, but I think in the end fails, in this book to atone with his dead father. In his attempt to do so, however, he completely demolishes the myth of rugged individualism that so characterized the contemporary image of the West. East versus West, civilization versus opportunity, is a theme at the heart of the American experience.

Stegner proved there is a big difference between builders and raiders in the history of the West. It was this theme that he explored further in *Beyond the Hundredth Meridian: John Wesley Powell and the Second Opening of the West.*

In 1878 Powell produced his famous *Report on the Lands of the Arid Region of the United States,* which continues to be one of the most contested views of the West in all of American history. Powell, like Stegner after him, argued that the West could only be understood by accepting its aridity and the conditions it imposed upon the number and activities of the people who came to live in it. Powell held that the rectangular surveys and rigid state and county lines that came into existence as the West was settled did not fit the irregularities of Western watersheds. Landscapes should determine jurisdictions, not politically expedient but completely artificial lines.

Stegner saw that behind Powell's general plan for the development of the West was something absolutely basic. What Powell possessed, Stegner wrote, was the "willingness to look at what was, rather than at what fantasy, hope, or private interest said should be."

In the end this was Powell's downfall. The human habit of distorting truth for personal gain that Powell put into relief beat him and defeated his ideas about the primacy of the watershed as the basic geophysical unit in the West. Myth, which was supported by Western politicians, said there was water for everyone and every use. Science, represented by Powell, said, "Wait a minute. Let's determine how much water there really is and what it can support." That suggestion, however, was a threat to boosters and mythmakers. In the end, science was defeated by myth.

A century and a half later, we are still doing exactly what Powell said should not be done to our own West. Ours is the same failure to accept limitations that has so utterly damaged so much of the United States west of the 100th meridian. And yet we fail to learn anything from the American example. Meanwhile, as predicted, the American deserts continue to advance northward – a fact that should be of great concern to those living on the Canadian prairies and on its fringes.

Stegner published *Angle of Repose* in 1971. As Jackson Benson notes in his biography of Stegner, the major motivating force behind the writing of *Angle of Repose* was Stegner's concern about the decline of civility and respect for knowledge in his own time.

It has been said that despite *The Big Rock Candy Mountain,* Stegner never really resolved his relationship with his father. But because of what Stegner wrote in *Angle of Repose,* I did. There is a passage near the ending of *Angle of Repose* where the main character, Lyman Ward, lies in bed, thinking, listening to the trucks labouring up the long grade on the highway near his Grass Valley home and wondering if he could possibly send for and thus forgive his unfaithful wife. "Wisdom," we hear Ward say, "... is knowing what you have to accept."

In this not-so-quiet darkness, hearing the diesel breaking its heart more and more faintly on the mountain grade, he lay wondering if he was man enough to be a bigger man than his grandfather – and to prove so through forgiveness. My father was a truck driver, and I imagined him behind the wheel of that diesel that was breaking its heart on that mountain grade.

Stegner was born in 1909, the same year my father was. I began to wonder at one point if he wasn't becoming something of a father figure to me. When I think about it now, however, it strikes me that he was more like a thoughtful uncle who, when I was ready to take the step into maturity, reintroduced me to my dead father in ways that allowed me to see him differently and to see myself differently as well. Finally, at 39, I was able not just to forgive but to actually understand, accept and love my father as I am sure I would have had he lived long enough for both of us to get through my rebellious years.

One of the most important things I learned from reading Wallace Stegner in this regard is that wisdom cannot exist where it has not been tempered by uncertainty. The memorable characters that Stegner created in novels like *Angle of Repose* all had serious doubts about what they thought they knew and how much about the world they really understood. The older they got, the less certain they were, and the more surprised they were that they were ever certain.

All of them, even at late stages in their lives, were, like Stegner, still trying to learn more about themselves, as well as about the people and the world around them. Because of these traits, Stegner's characters – like Stegner himself – often seem younger than the young people around them, who are often so very sure of themselves that they have become frozen enough in their opinions to be almost closed-minded.

In 1953, 33 years after leaving, Wallace Stegner and his wife, Mary, returned to Eastend, Saskatchewan, where Wallace wanted to do research for a memoir that would in part follow up on what he had written in *The Big Rock Candy Mountain*. What Stegner was really doing, however, was experimenting with what he later called the Doppler effect of history. Just as the sound of a train whistle changes pitch as it moves away from you, Stegner believed that history could be interpreted differently as one matured and viewed the past from a less immediate vantage in time.

Fearing that some of the older locals might remember his family, and in particular his father, Stegner kept a low profile and did not reveal his real name while he visited Eastend, a trip that also included a visit to his family's still-abandoned farm near the Montana border.

The resulting book, *Wolf Willow: A History, a Story, and a Memory of the Last Plains Frontier*, is now considered a classic in the growing genre of place-specific literature. Certainly it is far and away one of the most important books ever written on the Canadian prairies.

I will cite only a single passage from that book that

remains as relevant to me today as it was when I first read it while spending a year on a photographic project on the prairies nearly 30 years ago. It is the passage in which Stegner identifies what it is that so haunts him about his connection to his past and to this place:

> It is wolf willow, and not the town or anyone in it, that brings me home. For a few minutes, with a handful of leaves to my nose, I look across at the clay bank and the hills beyond where the river loops back on itself, enclosing the old sports and picnic ground, and the present and all the years between are shed like a boy's clothes on the bath-house bench.
>
> The perspective is what it used to be, the dimensions are restored, the senses are as clear as if they had not been battered with sensation for forty alien years. And the odd adult compulsion to return to one's beginnings is assuaged. A contact has been made, a mystery touched. For the moment, reality is made exactly equivalent with memory, and a hunger is satisfied. The sensuous little savage that I once was is still intact inside me....
>
> And he has a fixed suitably arrogant relationship with his universe, a relationship geometrical and symbolic. From his center of sensation and question and memory and challenge, the circle of the world is measured, and in that respect the years of experience I have loaded on my savage have not altered him.

Lying on a hillside where I once sprawled among the crocuses, watching the town herds and snaring May's emerging gophers, I feel how the world still reduces me to a point and then measures itself from me. Perhaps the meadowlark singing from a fence post – a meadowlark whose dialect I recognize – feels the same way. All points on the circumference are equidistant in him; in him all radii begin; all dimensions run through him; if he moves, a new geometry creates itself around him.

If you have experienced the openness and vastness of the prairies, you will realize that Wallace Stegner got this right.

Most of Stegner's books relate characters directly to place. One of the books in which he most articulately explores the personal relationship to place is entitled *The Sound of Mountain Water.* No matter where you live in the mountain West, the title itself will evoke place. It is in this book, also, that we see Stegner cast as reluctant voice for wilderness and for national parks.

Throughout the late 1960s, '70s and early '80s, Stegner was still guardedly optimistic about the ultimate fate of the West. Despite what careless people had done to what Stegner described as "a noble habitat," it remained difficult for him to be pessimistic. He maintained still that the West was "the native home of hope." His goal was to help create "a society to match the scenery." This is what he aspired to when he proclaimed the West "the geography of hope."

"There are some things wilderness can do for us," Stegner wrote. "That is the reason we need to put into effect, for its preservation, some other principle than the principles of exploitation or 'usefulness' or even recreation. We simply need that country available to us, even if we never do more than drive to its edge and look in. For it can be a means of reassuring ourselves of our sanity as creatures, a part of the geography of hope."

All of these notions he put into a famous letter – which came to be known as the Wilderness Letter – which he sent to David Pesonen at the Wildland Research Centre at the University of California at Berkeley on December 3, 1960. Of this letter, which is reprinted in *The Sound of Mountain Water*, Stegner later said: "Altogether, the letter, the labor of an afternoon, has gone further around the world than any other writings on which I have spent years ... Returning to the letter after 10 years, I find that my opinions have not changed. They have actually been sharpened by an increased urgency."

But, as the West changed, Stegner would later have serious reservations concerning just how much the West as a landscape was possessed of any kind of hope. But that chapter in Stegner's life comes later.

He held teaching posts at universities in Iowa, Utah and Wisconsin and at Harvard and Stanford. He also taught at the famous Bread Loaf Writers' Conference, held each summer near Middlebury, Vermont, which he attended eight times.

At Bread Loaf, Stegner established a close though sometimes tempestuous relationship with Robert Frost and initiated a lifelong friendship with Bernard DeVoto, who at the time was an influential monthly columnist in *Harper's Magazine*. He later wrote a remarkable biography of DeVoto, who, though living in the East, had become a very prominent Western writer. Bread Loaf was also the model for the creative writing program that Stegner later established at Stanford.

Wallace Stegner's perspectives on writing were captured in a small book published by his daughter-in-law Lynn Stegner in 2002. *On Teaching and Writing Fiction* offers exquisite personal insights into Stegner's teaching methods and fundamental ideas about writing as both craft and discipline. In this book, Stegner offers the view that writing is not merely craft but a means of becoming a better person.

Stegner disagreed vigorously with the view, still held in some circles today, that the true artist must always be an outsider and a renegade. Stegner once said that talents were as numerous as salmon eggs, and for the same reason. No amount of talent, in Stegner's estimation, granted the writer the right to be a jerk. Stegner made it clear in his teaching that he didn't like to use the term "artist" in reference to writing. "It has been adopted," he said, "by crackpots and abused by pretenders and debased by people with talent but no humility. In its capital-A form, it is the hallmark of that peculiarly repulsive sin of arrogance by which some practitioners of the arts retaliate for public neglect or compensate for personal inadequacy." Stegner maintained throughout his teaching life that it was the job of the serious writer to bring order where no order existed before. Stegner advised his students that the material available to the serious writer included the whole of his or her experience, actual or vicarious, and that the more that experience has hurt the writer – short of crippling them – the better.

Stegner taught that writing should not be viewed simply as an exercise in cleverness but a trial of understanding and a reflection on knowing and being. A good writer, Stegner maintained, is cocked and aimed like a gun and when he or she pulls the trigger should not be worrying about the calibre of the bullet or the special sound of the report. If he or she isn't a little dangerous to himself or herself and to others, then the writer is not living up to their calling.

Stegner also felt that a true writer never finished a book; one simply abandoned endless improvement to the ultimate fate of publication.

In the same way many of us here today in the Canadian Rockies have been affected by the work of Craig Richards, Wallace Stegner was much influenced by his friendship with Ansel Adams and often used photographic metaphors in describing the writer's craft. "One page or six hundred," he wrote, "a fiction is more than a well-carpentered entertainment. It is also more than the mirror in the roadway that Stendhal said it was. Because a good writer is not really a mirror; he is a lens. One mirror is like another, a mechanical reflector, but a lens may be anything from that which is in your Instamatic to what makes you handle your Hasselblad with reverence. Ultimately there is no escaping the fact that fiction is only as good as its maker. It sees only with the clarity that he is capable of, and it perpetuates his astigmatisms."

The list of the writers Stegner taught or influenced reads like the Who's Who of contemporary American literature. The list includes writers of the calibre of Barry Lopez, Ivan Doig, Gretel Ehrlich, Rick Bass, David Rains Wallace and Robert Stone. One of Stegner's favourites – and one of my favourite people of all time – was Terry Tempest Williams. Tempest Williams laments in her writing that our society is gradually teaching us to withhold our emotions in the face of the loss of so much that is meaningful in the world. She maintains that over time we have allowed ourselves to believe we should not care too deeply about what is important around us, because we are going to lose it anyway. She argues that we have become so used to hoarding our feelings that we have become inured to diminishment and loss. We have become so numb that when a landscape that matters to us is bought, sold or developed, clear-cut or grazed to rubble, or a hawk is shot and hung up by its feet on a barbed wire fence, our hearts are not broken because we no longer risk having strong emotional feelings about these matters. What kind of impoverishment, she asks, is it to withhold emotion, to restrain our natural connection to place just to appease our fears? She argues that a man or woman who reins in their heart when the body sings desperately for connection is only inviting more isolation and greater ecological decline. She claims that our lack of intimacy with each other is in direct proportion to our lack of intimacy with the land. She claims we have taken our love inside and abandoned the wild. This is not the West Williams wants. It is not the West Stegner wanted either.

William Kittredge also paid attention to Wallace Stegner and throughout his writing life built on StegWner's notion of the need to create a culture commensurate with place. In this, Kittredge maintains that keeping our language is far more important than we may know. Many parts of the mountain West have their own indigenous languages. To preserve what is essential about where and how we live, we must preserve these languages, for the loss of words can lead to the loss of the things those words stand for. The devaluation of words makes for the devaluation of the things words describe. With fewer words to describe the places that surround us, it becomes harder to justify saving them. As these places vanish from our direct experience, the need for a language to describe them vanishes as well. William Kittredge warns us that languages can decay and die. Once the language that people used to tell the story of who they are vanishes, their sense of self can be lost. People can become less than they were.

In his writing, Wes Jackson has urged Westerners to become native to where they live. In order to preserve even the possibility of an enduring sense of place, Jackson contends, we have to slow down our aimless, wandering pursuit of upward mobility at any cost and find a home, dig in and aim for some kind of lasting relationship with the ecological realities of the surrounding landscape. Jackson believes that we have to somehow reverse the Western frontier tradition of picking up and leaving the moment a place is no longer what we want it to be. We have to learn to stop running away. We have to stay and to stand up for where we live. We have to have confidence in what we are and what we can become. In this period of great change, we have to trust in the resilience of Western landscapes and Western people.

Biographer Philip Fradkin reports, however, that of all of the students who passed through Stegner's creative writing program at Stanford, Wendell Berry was by far his favourite. Their admiration for each other's work and principles, Fradkin reports, was sustained for 35 years.

Wendell Berry maintains that you can't know who you are unless you know where you are. Berry is troubled by the destructive precedent we inherited on this continent. He believes that by the time creatures have achieved consciousness, they should have become aware of the larger creation and how they fit into it. The failure to achieve this consciousness, Berry believes, will in the end exact a terrible penalty. The spirit of the creation will go out of them, they will become destructive and then the very earth will depart from them and go where they cannot follow.

My family members who were flooded out in Canmore and downstream in 2013, as well as flood victims I met in Manitoba in the summer of 2014, were saying pretty much the same thing. They cannot live in what their part of the West has now become. Because of changing hydro-climatic conditions, the West as they have known it has departed from them, and they can't follow. As his life advanced, this was how Stegner felt also. The West was turning into something he did not desire, while the West he loved was disappearing forever.

At the age of 60, Stegner soured on conservation politics, California's growth, teaching, hippie lifestyles and the war in Vietnam. Finding that he no longer desired social contact, he pulled up the drawbridge. He withdrew from the world to write. The next 20 years would be among his most productive. In this – as I have said – Stegner should be an inspiration to anyone who wonders if life can be meaningful with advancing age. But, while this was perhaps the most creative period in Stegner's life, it was also a period of profound trial. Stegner's life encompassed all the radical shifts in the West that spanned the 20th century. Stegner soon felt inundated, helpless and displaced, first from where he lived and then in the remainder of the West by the West's second great constant – the first being aridity, the second being change. The trouble started in Stegner's backyard.

In 1949 he and his wife Mary had built a home on seven acres of land in the Los Alto Hills, in what was then rural California, east of San Francisco. One morning, however, Wallace and Mary woke up to discover that where they lived was about to become Silicon Valley. What followed was what one biographer called a darkening of the Stegnerian persona. As Jackson Benson reports in his book *Down by the Lemonade Springs*, Silicon Valley was once the Santa Clara Valley, a delightful region of orchards and truck farms, as well as some vineyards. On a sunny day, one could see from high in the green foothills, above where Stegner had built his home, over a valley filled with trees to the glittering waters of San Francisco Bay just beyond. Now the air is dense with smog, the roads are choked with traffic and the farms are covered over by houses and industrial parks. Despite efforts to save it, the bay is badly polluted, a brown mess.

Benson reports that when the Stegners first built their house, they could look out in the other direction, across the hills behind them, and not see a single light flickering in the darkness. In the years just before Stegner died, the area around his modest ranch-style house became dotted with obscene "castles." Suddenly, over just a few years, the Stegners found themselves surrounded by huge mansions on mini-ranch-sized acreages, usually inhabited by one or two people or owned by absentee Asian entrepreneurs. That people would carve up his beloved foothills as an investment, not even bothering to live there, disturbed Stegner immensely.

In talking about the new West, but most particularly California, Stegner claimed there was a sense – to use Gertrude Stein's famous phrase about Oakland – that there is no longer any "there" there: no connection with history, no sense of connection with one's neighbours or sense of community, no feeling of connection with the land or reverence for the natural. In this, Stegner saw the erosion of the fundamental and founding values of the West. Stegner felt that whatever remained of the uniqueness of Western identity had been subsumed by mass culture. Modern Western individualism was now expressed almost solely through unrestrained corporatism. Whatever he had valued most in the West at one time was now irretrievably gone and could only be recovered in history and nostalgia.

In the face of radical change, Stegner began to feel less certain about the West's chances of creating "a society to match the scenery." Although he had once written, memorably, that the West was "hope's native home," he now admitted that he was not really hopeful about the West's future. Stegner declared that the West was no more the Eden he once thought it than the Garden of the World that the boosters and engineers tried to make it, and that neither nostalgia nor boosterism could any longer make a case for it as the geography of hope. The Eden, as he demonstrated by moving to Vermont, was now in the East. This in itself was an irony that, in Stegner's opinion, Westerners should not be able to bear. The fact was that while Vermont could heal, the dry West could not. Vermont became the place to go to find the things the West was settled for: space; the room to be yourself and grow. After *Crossing to Safety* – so to speak – Stegner made it clear that he held the West to be no longer a geography of hope but a geography of despair.

What Stegner chose in the end was a return to his beginnings. What he found in Vermont, as he had in Eastend, was a convergence of nature and human history. Why was that so attractive? Because, as he told an audience shortly before his death, "the business of studying the relations between places and people, and the ways in which people's living is conditioned by place, is one of the best ways I know of finding out about ourselves."

Stegner married Mary Stuart Page on September 1,

1934. They remained inseparably close for 59 years, until Wallace died from injuries suffered in a car accident on March 28, 1993. His ashes were spread in Vermont.

So what can we learn from Wallace Stegner about *our* West; which is to say, the mountain West in Canada and in particular the Bow Valley?

At the opening of this essay I proposed three fundamental tenets that, in my estimation, formed the foundation of Stegner's writing. Are they valid? Based on what Wallace Stegner taught us about *his* West, do these ideals still hold promise in *our* West? Here are my conclusions at this point in my life.

For the moment, at least, *our* West is different from *their* West. We still have a little room in ours. It really is true. It is not what we built but what we saved that really does make us unique. What we saved really does make where and how we live in the Canadian Rockies special. Fortunately, on one matter at least, Stegner is completely right. Our West is not fully made; Western culture and character are hard to define because they are still only half-formed. We continue to prove that we can love a place but still be dangerous to it. This suggests we are not worthy yet of what we have saved – but we still could be. We have reinvented ourselves once in our West – and there remains no reason we can't do it again. There are no obstacles except ones we have created ourselves. To be worthy of what we have saved we have to work to create – and keep on creating – a culture commensurate with, and reflective of, the remarkable qualities of the place in which we live.

At the moment at least, it appears we still have room

to move in creating the West we want. If we are able to create a society that matches the setting in which we live, then what we saved may very well save us. But if Wallace Stegner teaches us anything, it is this: we had better get moving while that room still exists.

PART TWO

Coming and Going

THE OTHER SIDE
OF PARADISE

Lynn Martel

I never planned to live in the mountains. But as soon as I found them, I knew I'd found home.

My first sight of Banff was through the window of a passenger train rolling from Calgary to Vancouver, which stopped briefly in Banff at dusk, then continued through the Rockies in pitch dark.

The following year, my sister, Daisy, left our hometown of Montreal with a friend who knew someone in Banff. Our father's Air Canada job as an instrument technician granted us several free flights a year, and Daisy and I had mastered the art of flying standby on the slimmest of budgets. I can still hear her first phone call home.

"There's mountains everywhere!"

Three months later, I was couch surfing in the tiny one-bedroom apartment she shared with a roommate.

Partying at Banff's hottest nightclub, Silver City (now Aurora), I scanned the dance floor for cute guys.

"You've got to be kidding," I scoffed. "These people are wearing *jean jackets*."

I was mortified. I was from Montreal, where a girl's wardrobe and fashion sense were competitive sports from the age of 11. Banff was so hick! Worse, while beer and wine were sold at corner dépanneurs in Montreal even on holidays, prior to the 1988 Olympics you couldn't purchase alcohol on Sunday in Alberta.

Despite the cultural faux pas, I enjoyed Banff. I went bathing in a natural hot spring (since barricaded) on Sulphur Mountain. Everyone was relaxed and friendly, and when I returned in winter people remembered me and welcomed me warmly. Several visits later, in May 1984, as soon as my semester studying creative writing at Concordia University ended, I was back. I thought that if I found a job I'd stay the summer. Within days, I moved in with a cute Silver City waiter, Joe, and his two roommates in a cozy three-bedroom basement. Pretty soon the landlords upstairs requested we find other accommodations since our late-night lifestyle was understandably incompatible with their impending parenthood. Joe and I downsized to two bedrooms and just one roommate. For three years, we were inseparable – the latter part of that period as husband and wife. The entire time I did my best to downplay his heavy drinking and abusive behaviour, as 20-something girls idealistically do. Days before my 26th birthday, three apartments and much agonizing later, I left him.

By then, however, I was completely in love with

mountain town living. While I appreciated the Banff Centre's urbanesque weekly foreign film showings, in those pre–Much Music or Internet days, I loved feeling isolated from city life and the unquestionable expectation of working 50 weeks a year in an office cubicle with a rigid dress code – expectations that had caused me considerable anxiety. In Banff, working service industry jobs with my peers felt liberating. We were young, what more did we need?

My first job was at the funky Banff Book & Art Den, where a spiral staircase led to the second floor housing the classics, a spicy lingerie corner and a candle making machine whose scent permeated everything. There I discovered *The Canadian Rockies Trail Guide,* page after black-and-white page beckoning with promises of grand adventure. Whenever Brian Patton or Bart Robinson – its mythical authors who'd hiked every trail in the Mountain Parks – visited, I was star-struck. One day, a real celebrity dropped by; a striking woman wearing silver and turquoise jewelry bought a hardcover copy of *I Ching.* Her credit card signature read Joni M. Mitchell. I still have the carbon.

Growing up in Montreal, for adventure we'd take shortcuts to school (nobody's parents, even those with cars, drove kids *anywhere*), hopping backyard fences and skirting back alley dumpsters. Once a summer, we'd pile aboard my grandfather's station wagon – Daisy and me in the back cargo section – for a day trip to Vermont. Enjoying the ruffle chips and cream soda special treat, I'd watch other families set up tents and build campfires, wishing our family camped overnight. Thankfully, our parents sent us to Girl Guide Camp for two weeks several summers running in the Laurentians. Barely an hour from what was then Canada's largest city, I yearned for a lake free of cottages, motorboats or people; just nature, unfettered, unpopulated.

The Canadian Rockies Trail Guide led me to dozens of such lakes.

I became manager at Mountain Magic Sportswear, the trendiest outdoor shop in Banff. I bought a mountain bike on layaway; this exciting new invention had fat tires that rolled over dirt trails. Like other Eastern 20-somethings, who comprised most of Banff's summer staff – a fraction of whom would stay on through ski season – I had no concept of wilderness travel. Many days I explored alone, long before cellphones or GPS or bear spray. My bike was my ticket to freedom, and with every kilometre pedalled, my confidence grew. On one trip my friend Judy Smith (now Smith-Musselman) and I pedalled from Banff Avenue via the Spray River (now closed) to Bryant Creek. Stashing our bikes at the base of Assiniboine Pass, we hiked, finally reaching Naiset Cabins at dusk. As I collected creek water, the full moon illuminated the flow like shimmering mercury. It was pure magic. I never wanted to leave.

I learned to ski at Lake Louise with my friend Niki Lepage, who also took me up Rundle for my first scramble. Niki knew how to rock climb and ski across glaciers, and I wondered if I could ever learn the skills necessary to do such wildly adventurous things. From that summit, the peaks stretched forever in every direction, and I wondered what lay down every valley and over every pass. Over time, with fellow adventurers and especially adventuresses, I hiked to backcountry huts without electricity or running water, our relationships strengthening along with our endurance. I met climbers who described sleeping on portaledges attached to sheer cliffs and partied at a fundraising bash for Peter Arbic, Troy Kirwan and Barry Blanchard to go climb K2, even though I wasn't sure where K2 was. I was introduced to ski touring on the near-deserted untracked slopes of Rogers Pass and visited Nelson and Revelstoke, where the real ski bums lived, and where houses were cheaper than Banff's. For all of us living the mountain life, finding a place to live that fit our earnings was an ongoing challenge. Many of us who shared small apartments with roommates whose company we didn't always enjoy couldn't help but be envious of our Revelstoke friends, who only needed to work one job to afford to buy actual houses with backyards. But then, Revy did seem isolated, and the job choices were certainly limited compared to the work available in the more accessible Bow Valley.

One summer day, cruising single track near Heart Mountain, I braked hard and stood gripping my handlebars, facing a black bear and her cub-of-the-year just five metres from me. I readied myself for her charge; I deserved it. The dark chocolate brown sow paused then disappeared into the willows while the creamy white cub scrambled up a tree. Sensing her departure, it backpedalled down and tore off after her. A minute later Niki rode up, but it was over. Nothing, I learned, was more fascinating, mysterious or precious than nature.

Backcountry travel led me to understand how every living thing on the planet is connected to the great web of life, including us humans, despite our natural tendency to foul our own nest.

Switching to waitressing for better money, I embraced hiking/biking/skiing by day, serving dinners at night. I bought a little Toyota pickup for $1,000 and my world expanded. I worked part-time at a back-alley shop selling used skis and politically incorrect T-shirts, which morphed into Rude Boys, *the* Rockies hub for the exciting new sport of snowboarding.

In autumn 1992, I sublet my apartment and lived in Maui for two months, working illegally at a mountain bike/surf rental shop. When I had first moved to Banff, Daisy, who always made friends more easily than I did, was already there. I felt a need to go somewhere on my own, without anyone paving the way for me. I felt proud of myself for finding a place to live and a job in Maui, an unknown place, even though I had no intention of staying. I'd packed along the latest issue of *Powder Magazine* bearing a cover image of a 70-ish woman riding a tram, holding a pair of Kneissl skis much taller than her. While beach life was pleasant, that image punctuated for me that the Rockies life I'd embraced was really a distinct and vibrant culture of its own – mountain culture – and it was rich with its own stories of skiers, mountain bikers and climbers.

Since I was 11, I'd always kept a journal. Writing about my life has always been a natural urge, like breathing. Dating back to my teenage years, when I began experiencing periods of depression, the act of releasing my emotions onto the page had always been a salve, an outlet by which I could shed my struggles and face the world for another, hopefully better day. Through my painful, tumultuous and often dark years with Joe, writing down what I was experiencing had helped me gain clarity and eventually the strength to leave him. From a young age, in the back of my mind I saw myself as being capable of writing a book, although I knew nothing about how one went about beginning, let alone accomplishing, such a thing. While it was just for me, and not for any audience, writing a journal was something I could never not do.

Once home from Maui, I set up a garage sale drafting table, bar stool and electric typewriter in my living room. I mailed stories to magazines, received rejection letters back and saw my ideas written by other writers. Finally, *Bike Magazine* assigned me a destination piece about mountain biking in Banff. When the issue arrived in my mailbox, the full-body rush that washed over me was the most profound combination of excitement and pride I've ever felt.

Committing to writing several days a week in balance with outdoor days, I learned that restaurant jobs were as disposable as many of my employers made me feel. One manager fired me after a customer's chair caused a decorative light to become unplugged; another, a Japanese manager, hit me on my back, open-handed, for breaking a restaurant rule by snacking in the kitchen midway through a long shift. I charged him with assault; he earned a conditional discharge and kept his job. I found myself unemployed and in debt in job-lean

April. The court experience was not one I'd want to repeat. Ironically, many years later that judge would seek my advice about writing his book.

In 1993 I moved to Canmore, where basement apartments were plentiful and much cheaper, and where *hick* took on new meaning compared to glamorous Banff; one friend called Canmore "Bug Tussle." While I was waitressing at the Sherwood House, Hollywood came to town to film *Last of the Dogmen*. Like many locals, I was hired as an extra for five dollars an hour. Working on set in a coal field now labelled Cary Street, I observed the tediously slow filmmaking process and typed up an article describing how I felt like live wallpaper, then delivered the pages to the *Canmore Leader* office, upstairs from the Coffee Mine. Editor Carol Picard ran every word, filling pages one and two of the Community section. I was over the moon!

Working part-time as a bus hostess for Canadian Mountain Holidays, I accompanied heli-skiing guests to and from lodges in BC's big Selkirk and Monashee mountains. The guests taught me that disposable income is no measure of anyone's true character. Occasionally I was lucky to sit with senior mountain guides, especially Lloyd "Kiwi" Gallagher, who kept me spellbound with stories of early heli-skiing and climbing in the 1960s and '70s. By then my married and partnered friends were buying homes in Canmore, some of them opting for condos in Benchlands, a new neighbourhood that in those days was accessed only by a dirt road from Harvie Heights. My peers became the generation that populated Canmore's growing neighbourhoods and schools. While I've always wished I might someday meet a man who would be my partner, having survived a miserable marriage and a demanding boss through my 20s, motherhood held no allure; I'd had enough serious responsibility putting others first. I also understood instinctively that as a creative person who *needs* a fair bit of alone time, I could not be happy being the parent who stayed home with the kids while their father was out working and pursuing outdoor adventures, as I was witnessing among my friends. I had my own identity to nurture, adventures to pursue.

And so many stories to write.

Looking back, it's astounding how rapidly technology changed our little mountain world. VCRs – and extreme sports videos and antics – became ubiquitous. I watched Joe Josephson type his *Waterfall Ice* guidebook on a curious new computer screen in his apartment above Second Story Books on Canmore's Main Street. I bought a used computer and learned to cut and paste. "In a few years everyone will have computers in their homes," my brother-in-law, Al, said, although I couldn't quite imagine how or why.

I grew my library, reading the Rockies writers – Sid Marty, Jon Whyte, Bob Sandford, Ben Gadd, Chic Scott, Ruth Oltmann, Cyndi Smith – to know my mountain world deeper through their words and experiences and ideas, to understand how the mountain landscape inspired them to write about this place, in their time. I realized that while the Rockies' early history was well documented, very little was being written about the world I lived in. After 18 months in Canmore, I moved back to Banff; I was a snowboarder living in a climbers' town, and I felt a bit out of place and lonely in Canmore. It was a good move for my writing – at that time in my life I recognized lots more for me to write about in Banff. The Banff *Crag & Canyon* focused on skiing as business, while my friends worked as ski patrollers, avalanche specialists and mountain guides. *Crag* editor Dave Rooney accepted my pitch to write six articles about behind-the-scenes jobs at all six Rockies ski hills, for $30 apiece; with the expense of driving from Fortress to Jasper, I lost money on the bargain. But Rooney was pleased and suggested I write a snowboarding column, so, for two winters, The Blind Side described learning to take air, hitchhiking etiquette and, following a heartbreaking accident at Fortress, backcountry avalanche awareness, a burgeoning topic for the public. Through those years, I spent my winters snowboarding in fresh powder to a soundtrack of Green Day and Nirvana with my good friend Maria Hawkins. A naturally gifted athlete who had competed as a cyclist in the 1992 Barcelona Olympics, Maria pushed me to become a better snowboarder than I would have been on my own. Both of us had previously been skiers, and as unmarried and childfree 30-somethings enjoying a sport more often associated with a much younger demographic, we had chairlift conversations about bigger themes that inspired most of the topics I wrote about.

Magazine articles followed in *Avenue West, Explore* and *Fresh & Tasty*, a woman's snowboard mag, and *The Wildlife*, Banff's hip monthly paper that celebrated the culture of its colourful under-35 workforce. Postcards from Paradise ensued, a biweekly column commenting on basement dwelling, "things I've learned to love about our tourists" and sometimes questioning the less glamorous aspects of our mountain world, each instalment delivered on floppy disks to the *Crag* office, as dial-up was excruciatingly slow. One of those columns, written in response to a cheeky piece *Crag* editor Sherri Zickefoose had freelanced for *Rolling Stone,* identifying Banff as the STD capital of Canada, was pulled by publisher Sandra Santa Lucia. With umpteen bars in a three-block radius, countless happy hours and low-paid service industry workers crammed six to a two-bedroom apartment, if Banff was widely known to young people as a party town, I argued, it was because we'd created it.

One day, chasing a story about the Banff Springs and Chateau Lake Louise hotels resurrecting their professional mountain guide programs, I interviewed Bob Sandford over drinks at the Mount Royal pub. The encounter marked the beginning of a rich and enduring friendship, as he became – and remains – my most encouraging mentor. At his urging, I joined the Alpine Club of Canada, and its Mountain Culture Committee, which he chaired. In addition to introducing me to some wonderful backcountry partners, the Alpine Club connection ultimately led to me writing nine historical/biographical booklets, recording the stories of those whose contributions helped shape our unique mountain world. I even grew the confidence to learn how to rock climb and participate in mountaineering adventures on some respectable Rockies peaks, albeit by the easiest routes. I much prefer exploring to riding lifts, so backcountry ski touring fully replaced snowboarding, and remains my favourite winter activity.

By 1999, though, I couldn't serve another table. I loved the customers but had no patience left for the service industry work atmosphere. Spotting an ad in the *Canmore Leader* for a full-time reporter, I applied. Despite my lack of a journalism degree, editor Dave Burke hired me on the strength of my columns in the *Crag* and my deep local knowledge. With Daisy, and her husband Al, and my newborn niece, Devyn, living in Canmore, when friends offered me their one-bedroom basement apartment I moved again, ready to give Canmore another shot – my 14th apartment in 16 years (most of them basements). Only half of those moves had been my choice. One landlord couple, long-time Banffites who lived upstairs, had complained about the sound of my roommate turning the water tap on and off.

"Well," I'd shrugged. "You and your friends kept me up until two a.m. the other night with your loud music."

"But that's our privilege as landlords," she'd quipped. With the support of Alberta's landlord/tenant laws, I'd packed up and moved before I owed her one more dime of my hard-earned tips. By contrast, my Canmore basement granted me six mostly peaceful years, disrupted only by realtors parading buyers through my home as it switched hands twice with me living there. Having my newly retired parents move to Canmore in 2001 made living there feel complete.

Working as a reporter at the *Canmore Leader* alongside Rob Alexander, photographer Pam Doyle and David Burke was engaging, challenging, at times draining and endlessly interesting and rewarding. Meeting weekly deadlines taught us all discipline and incredible flexibility for grasping diverse subject matter. But working 45- to 50-hour weeks on a $21,000 salary (never a cent of overtime, and no allowance for our "mandatory" vehicles) took its toll. I worked part-time at the Banff Upper Hot Pools, doling out towels to bathers. During quiet times, I joked that I was paid more to read newspapers than I was to write one.

Meanwhile, Carol Picard started a new paper, the *Rocky Mountain Outlook* – full colour, modern, smart and free. I continued to write my Postcards from Paradise column for the *Leader*, and in one instalment welcomed the *Outlook*, but publisher Shari Bishop squashed it. After 26 months, I quit. Office morale was in the toilet, and anything had to be better than where I was.

It was a blessing. Freelancing with outdoor magazines, and with the *Outlook*, I found my niche, writing about the Bow Valley and the Rockies' rich and layered and exciting mountain culture. The more stories I pursued, the deeper I understood how mountain people live by the seasons, shaped by the landscape: the forests and the wildlife, the glaciers, the high peaks, deep valleys, turquoise lakes and surging rivers. Horsemen and mountaineers and entrepreneurs and storytellers who shape their own stories as they capture others' stories; everyone's stories are bound to the mountains like a solid snowpack, while each is unique as a snowflake. The distinctiveness and vibrancy of our own Rockies culture unfolded before me, each story opening the next, revealing dynamic, accomplished, creative, smart, fascinating people all congregated in the Bow Valley. I truly felt I was living in exceptionally "interesting times." I was honoured to write obituaries for Bruno Engler, Sam Evans, Bud Brewster and Hans Gmoser, to interview champion athletes and dedicated conservationists and refugees from Sierra Leone. On the other hand, writing an obit for Karen McNeill, a climber I'd known for years, was torture.

"You're so lucky to live here," visitors would say. "No," I always replied. "It's a choice." I learned that, for me, living in the mountains was never about the view out my window, never about the perfect ski run or my most challenging climb. Living in the mountains has always been about the view into my soul, the expression of my spirit and feeling connected to the natural wilderness landscape. And writing about the mountain world became my place in the world.

On a FAM (slang for *familiarization*) tour, I was blessed to visit Andy Russell at his "Hawk's Nest" cabin near Waterton Lakes National Park, where I asked him, "If it's okay for you to live here on this mountaintop, how come you don't support others building homes in this area?"

"Because they don't know how to behave," Russell growled. "They build houses that are way too big. They don't know how to respect the land, they don't know how to respect the wildlife."

I understood; I lived in Canmore.

At first, the changes crept gradually. Another stop light. Safeway came; locally owned Marra's closed. Another stop light. Another golf course. Another development, another miner's house torn down, another perfectly sound 1970s bungalow replaced by an up-scale condo consuming every square foot of the lot it occupied, only to sit empty with the heat running 11 months of the year. Along with the nausea I felt think-ing about how many trees were needlessly cut down and how much energy was consumed to create something so decadent, I felt bruised by the attitude of entitlement that fuelled those status-symbol "weekend homes." Whatever happened to the simple cottage? Years earlier, Bob Sandford had said to me: "Watch out for Canmore." At the time, I lacked the awareness and insight to im-agine what he meant.

In 2006 my new landlords increased my rent and blasted the TV in their living room above my bedroom at six a.m. Friends offered me a great one-bedroom basement for the same $600 a month I'd been paying, so I moved *again*. The most visually pleasing walk-out I'd ever rented, it was hell at night, when the upstairs neighbours walked in heavy shoes on the hardwood floor and had drunken fights and then made up in their bedroom, which was unfortunately above mine. By day, thankfully, the apartment granted me a tranquil home to assemble my first book, *Expedition to the Edge*. After two years there, the phone rang. "We're going to sell the place, you have three months to move." I phoned around and mass emailed. Finally, an acquaintance of-fered a one-bedroom walk-out, $1,000 a month, plus utilities. Whoa! I kept looking, placing ads in the paper, on community corkboards. Nothing even close to being affordable. I felt rejected by my own town.

I was exhausted. I just wanted a home that I wouldn't

be pushed out of at the landlord's whim. My parents helped me borrow to buy a three-bedroom townhouse, 1,050 square feet, 350 on each floor. I lived upstairs, where 700 square feet provided me a bedroom, an office, kitchen and living area, while I rented out the walk-out ground floor studio, becoming landlord to a procession of delightful young workers from Nova Scotia, Czech Republic, Japan, Nepal and Quebec. I couldn't really afford it, but if a place to live in Canmore was going to cost half my income, I might as well be putting it into a mortgage.

And my career progressed. I was invited to present at the Banff Mountain Book Festival, and several of my photos were displayed in a Whyte Museum exhibit. I curated a *History of Skiing in Canmore* exhibit for Canmore's museum. While I had always understood and accepted that writing was an appetizer or famine profession, the variety and range of the learning experiences it provided me, coupled with a steady stream of thanks from neighbours and strangers at the grocery store and coffee shops encouraged me to continue. I'd watched talented writers give up on their gift, saying it paid too little to earn a living. I hung on. I watched many leave the Bow Valley, saying housing was too expensive. I hung on. The valley was my home, my whole life. I would work harder. Earn more.

Then the crash hit.

Overnight, the same realtors and developers whose ads made it possible for the *Outlook* to employ me (while simultaneously driving Canmore's property values) cut their ads, and my already tight income was slashed by 65 per cent. On the upside, I was amused by the sudden surge of weekend homeowners' classifieds advertising their previously unrented basement studios with marble countertops for $1,200 a month, as if that's what every grocery store clerk was clamouring for. I had no trouble keeping my studio rented to young workers, but not at the amount I needed to balance my expenses.

Over three decades, the mountains taught me invaluable lessons. Backcountry adventures taught me how to keep moving no matter how tired, wet, cold, hungry or sore I was. From mountain biking, rock climbing and ski touring, I discovered I could do anything if I started at the beginning, practised the basics and put in the mileage. I learned to manage my discomfort with exposure well enough to rock climb on steep, even overhanging cliffs. I learned to trust my instincts. Living in small rural towns taught you to be nice to your neighbour because you'd actually get to know each other and you might need an egg someday. I grew to love the feeling of being harboured in the bosom of the larger Bow Valley/Rockies community. I'm blessed to experience the feeling of making other mountain people happy with the stories I write.

Historically, living in small mountain towns such as Banff and Canmore meant letting go of urban conveniences – fewer choices at the grocery store, fewer options for medical care or for employment. Those who committed to living in these towns did so because we felt we had everything we needed, with a couple of city runs a year. We could hike, ski and climb without needing six-figure incomes. Life moved slower, potlucks trumped highbrow catering. A person's virtue was measured by their neighbourliness and their volunteer ethic, not the sticker price of their SUV or the architecture of their 3,000-square-foot "weekend" home. Living with less meant a life brimming with riches. And did it really matter if the liquor store wasn't open on Sundays?

Shifting baseline syndrome suggests, rather accurately, that the generation born today will accept the world as they enter it as how it should be, without any awareness or nostalgia for how it used to be. Newcomers to the Bow Valley today enter a "mountain retreat" of 12,000 full-time and 5,800 part-time residents, relative to Calgary as a city of 1.2 million. In 1980, Canmore as Bug Tussle was home to less than 3,000, while Calgary's population was 560,000. For those who appreciated Canmore for its ball diamond with weather-faded bleachers that occupied the giant field where Save-On, Canadian Tire and Safeway all stand now, Bug Tussle has morphed into Big Hustle, complete with road rage and condo boards that unfathomably forbid hanging clean wet laundry outdoors. Over a couple of short decades, Canmore invited the world to its great little "paradise" but neglected to carve out living space for the willing workers servicing that comfortable living as grocery store cashiers, gas jockeys, baristas, retail clerks and hotel cleaners. The campground was privatized and subsequently denied to essential seasonal staff. With the construction of Elevation Place – so tirelessly advocated by Dung Nguyen, who nurtured Canmore's world-class youth climbing team from scratch while his Vsion gym doubled as his home for years – Nguyen was refused his chance to manage it. Everyone knew his business wouldn't survive the competition.

Consume, compete, conquer.

While Canmore has so many charms – riverside paths, hiking trails, rock-climbing areas, cross-country skiing trails, a kick-ass folk music festival and a community of brilliant, talented, inspiring individuals – for many who chose it to be home because houses were unassuming and affordable, and because nobody cared if their cutlery matched or if their skis were a few seasons old, it's become unrecognizable, and, for some, unlivable. While we appreciate the inspiration Canmore's abundance of world-class athletes and overachieving adventurepreneurs provide us, for many who aren't Type A's, Canmore can easily feel pushy, aggressive, demanding, as unrelenting as the drone of highway traffic has become. And, at times, overwhelming. My stress escalated. I could not write fast enough to cover my cost of living, particularly housing. Extreme financial stress is not something I would wish on anyone. I spiralled; anxiety escalated to depression. I felt like the world's biggest failure. How could I ever live up to anyone's expectations of me? How could I ever measure up, contribute enough to belong in this world?

I sank. The bottom loomed.

Do what you love and the money will follow. Well, I would not recommend anyone choose writing as a profession. At the same time, I could not trade being a writer for any amount of money. But, so far, after more than 20 years and despite working full-time hours, I have not yet figured out how to make more than hand-to-mouth money writing the stories I see as being essential, necessary to who we are in this place. When

Canmore sucked away from me the very thing I need to be who I am – a quiet, low-cost place to live with space for me to work at my desk in solitude, ideally separate from my bedroom – then I knew what I had to trade was Canmore. On November 25, 2012, I loaded everything into a U-Haul and drove two hours west to the edge of the Rockies, to Golden, BC. With my family all still in Canmore, it was, no contest, the toughest decision of my life.

I divided my time between calm, productive weeks in Golden, and hectic, inspiring days in Canmore. Ironically, living in Golden made it possible for me to continue to write about the Rockies and the Bow Valley, and the amazing people who contribute to our very special mountain culture. Maintaining and growing my connections to a wonderful community of accomplished people throughout the mountains blesses me with a life that's full, endlessly interesting and immensely rewarding.

I felt I'd come full circle, proudly renting my Canmore condo to several Bow Valley service industry workers who aren't stressed sharing such small quarters, while in Golden I rented a small two-bedroom house on several acres for the price of a bedroom with a shared bath in Canmore. It wasn't glamorous or exactly to code, but it was perfect. Nobody wears headsets in Golden's grocery store, where most faces are familiar. I met great people through volunteer groups and acquaintances I knew before I arrived. And I cleared my head enough to plan ahead, steer my career and benefit from my creativity. Although I wasn't great at it, I loved having my own little veggie garden.

How long until Golden is assimilated? Its three-hour distance from Calgary renders it difficult for people to commute daily to and from Golden, where job options are limited and locals proudly drive cars worth less than their mountain bikes and nobody compares the granite their countertops are made of. The local music scene is outstanding. Some Goldenites wish their town was busier, but I tell them to be careful what you wish for. You might get it.

As the months, then two and a half years passed, Golden didn't feel like home. Driving back and forth to Canmore several times a month began to wear me out in many ways. Thirty years' worth of friends are not casually replaced, and everyone I'm close to – my parents, my sister, my best friends – are in Canmore. Loneliness visited, and some days that two-hour drive seemed so much longer than it is. Bit by bit, day after day, I began to know deeply that my home, and my community, is in Canmore. It took nearly three years, but my stress is all gone, and I believe I have learned how to manage the challenges that are guaranteed to test me in the future. Four days before the deadline for this essay, I moved everything back to Canmore.

While my work plate is steadily full, the pay scale ranges wildly from meagre to generous – the former, of course, being far more plentiful. While on paper my situation hasn't really changed much, for me the value of my condo has increased substantially as Canmore's rental situation for lower-income workers is as tight as ever. I am now able – still without gouging my tenants – to rent the upper two-bedroom apartment of my condo for an amount that makes it affordable for me to live in the ground-floor studio, allowing me to decide to return to Canmore without the stress of looking for a home. Unfortunately, in doing so I've inflicted that ordeal on the wonderful couple who has been living there for two and half years. It's a full-circle decision I do not feel good about.

For my part, cooking, eating, sleeping, reading and working full-time in just 325 square feet presents a whole new challenge as I embrace my 18th home in 31 years, but at least this time the choice is mine. And I get to paint in colours I like, and there's space outside for a veggie garden. I feel whole again to be living in the same town as my family and my closest friends and this truly amazing community, especially my fellow mountain writers and backcountry partners who make me feel valued and appreciated. I am so grateful for all the hugs I've received since I moved back.

After three decades in the Bow Valley, I really do hope to someday have a home I can live in for more than a couple of years. But at the same time, it's been interesting to mark the progression of my life, and especially my writing, from one apartment to the next. I am immensely proud of everything I've accomplished so far, and extremely grateful for all the support and encouragement I've received from wonderful people.

And I've begun working on my next book, about the glaciers of my home, the Canadian Rockies. I'm ready for the next adventure.

RETURNING TO MY SENSES

Jamey Glasnovic

I have heard it said that where you grew up was your parents' home, where you choose to live as an adult is *your* home. As an adult you must find a unique place that reflects what is important to you, a place that is comfortable and provides inspiration. It is no easy task. Some people are perfectly happy in, and suited to, the very neighbourhood they grew up in. Some people follow their work, and that takes them to the right place and they never think about it again. For many of us, the journey is not as straightforward.

I have loved this place since I first passed through here in 1995. I was on a bicycle, heading to Vancouver from Calgary; the Bow Valley was one of many scenic marvels in what was a thorough introduction to the mountain West. Something from that brief encounter stuck with me. It wasn't the town of Canmore or Banff or Lake Louise that caught my attention; it was the magnificent landscape, the way it rises up from the high prairie east of Canmore and then keeps on rising. There are prairie people, there are ocean people and there are city people. Everybody has a place they feel most at ease in. I am a mountain person, and though I only first visited these mountains two decades ago, I was a mountain person long before I first set eyes on them. Before that, they existed in my imagination. In the Bow Valley, my imagination became reality.

My friend Bob Sandford and I often talk about the importance of place, of being connected to your surroundings in a way that has purpose and meaning. I am drawn to his observation that it is not what small-town folks build that gives them a sense of community but what they save. Unique history, the local environment and close personal relationships are what make living in a small town worthwhile for most, and the erosion of this sense of place is often brought on by rapid and poorly regulated growth, usually initiated by outside interests.

It remains a fundamental part of the human experience to belong, and although there are some common themes, the criteria for what that means varies for each individual. The Bow Valley attracts people who feel they cannot live comfortably without a healthy dose of "outside" in their day-to-day lives. That is the reason, more than any other, that *I* came here. For those who merely visit, it is enough to come on vacation in the summertime, or for a long weekend in winter. But the growing interest paid to our little slice of heaven lately is not without consequence. In Canmore, we are no longer a small town but have graduated to miniature-city status.

This is not an official designation you would find on any sign or map, but that's how it feels, and the pros and cons of that change are impossible to ignore.

On the one hand, we are a rich community, and have grown from a comparatively modest 3,000 people in the mid-'80s to something like 16,000 full- and part-time residents today. The last of the coal mines closed in the late '70s, and now tourism is our trade. As a result, there are some truly great restaurants and plenty of shopping and lots to do – even if traipsing around in the wilderness is not your particular cup of tea. It is, however, extremely expensive to live here, even if you do manage to find an affordable apartment, condo or duplex. Single-family detached home? Not unless you've got three quarters of a million dollars to spend. And don't even get me started about the zoo this place turns into on a warm sunny weekend in the summer.

Still, the Canadian Rocky Mountains and their ability to stir the senses have remained in my consciousness for 20 years, and Canmore has been my home for 10 of those. A UNESCO World Heritage Site, the collection of national and provincial parks that surround Canmore is one of the largest protected areas on earth, and is home to grizzly bears, wolves, black bears and cougars, in addition to countless other animal and plant species. Some of them rare and/or endangered. The parks are also an integral piece in the puzzle that is the Yellowstone to Yukon Conservation Initiative, which is an attempt to connect and protect additional habitat in the 3200-kilometre window between Yukon and Wyoming. These mountains make up the spine of the continent, and in addition to being rugged and scenic, these headwaters are now being recognized as extremely important not only to the local ecologies that they sustain but to all the communities downstream as well because of the reliable water supply they provide.

But Banff National Park, the first national park in Canada, is also the most heavily visited in the Canadian national park system, with three to four million visitors a year. It has a major highway and national railway running through the centre of it, in addition to the two towns (Banff and Lake Louise) situated within its boundaries. In the exceedingly difficult balance between conservation and reasonable use, between business interests and wildlife, we are at ground zero in the Bow Valley. It is a relationship that can inspire and frustrate in equal measure.

When my friend and fellow local author Stephen Legault asked me if I wanted to be a part of a group project he was working on called *Imagine This Valley*, I immediately said, "Yes, of course, send me the info and we'll figure something out." But the truth is, in that moment I didn't have time to hear about it, think about it or plan on what kind of contribution I wanted to make. Like many of my colleagues, I don't just write. I also have another job to help pay my bills, and that job was in the process of kicking my ass. To be honest, I didn't have the energy for anything else. Imagining this valley would have to wait.

Fortunately, Stephen had a lot of other writers to corral, and there was time for me to get my act together. It is, of course, a great idea: eloquent and passionate people reflecting on the place that gives them so much inspiration. After our first exchange about this book, I would occasionally get an email from Stephen, gently inquiring about my progress. The answer was always the same: "It's on my 'to do' list." In reality, I wasn't really doing anything about it. Even with the simple directive "write whatever you want," I didn't know what to write, which is a bit odd, because I had just published a whole book on a similar subject. *Lost and Found: Adrift in the Canadian Rockies* is 100,000 words about my experience in the Rockies that I had spent six years researching and agonizing over before eventually seeing it in print, and here I was having trouble coming up with an additional 1,500 words. I was experiencing the worst writer's block of my life.

Eventually, it dawned on me that it wasn't too many words that were required but rather not enough. After all, how do you summarize your experience of a place when the experience of that place is ongoing and changing all the time? Even with a book under my belt, it turns out there was so much I still wanted to say. Stephen, in one of his last emails to me, asked, as a prompt in the attempt to get things rolling, "What is it about this place that attracted you? Why do you stay? What makes it easy? What makes it hard?" These are excellent questions. Why do I think of this place so much still? Why do I dream about the peaks and hidden valleys and distant trails that make up so much of my own experience here? Why do I let the towns, crowded with people so much of the year, get on my nerves so much? Why not do something else? Go somewhere else? Start over?

The "same old same old" on rapid repeat is the plight of those toiling away in the mini-city, but then this place takes my breath away all over again and I can't imagine living anywhere else.

Often, it is Mount Lawrence Grassi in the early morning sunshine in March and April that gets me. The sun is at a perfect angle at this time of year, low yet bright, as if it is slowly gearing up for summer. The snow is also gone from the valley bottom by then but is still draped over the tops of all the mountains around town. The air remains crisp in the early morning but carries with it the promise of afternoon warmth. Walking the 30 metres from my condo to the Fas Gas for a coffee, the mountain towers above, and it is impossible to avoid being awestruck, even after a decade of seeing the same sight over and over.

It turns out this place doesn't care about my problems or distractions. It doesn't even care when I ignore it, neglect it or take it for granted. When I'm ready to come back to my senses, when I'm ready to go outside again, there is always a stunning landscape right outside my door, waiting to be explored. Or simply admired, if a couple of minutes is all I have to spare. Why do I think of this place so much after all these years?

Maybe I do that because it is home.

COFFEE AT THE TEMPLE

Maria Gregorish

Taking a deep breath, I push the heavy glass doors at the Canmore Legion and enter.

The sunny March morning slips off my shoulders and I am plunged, shivering, inside the restaurant.

I hesitate on the threshold, put off by the windowless room, by the walls covered in wood panels. It looks like a sunken ship and I don't feel like scuba diving.

And there's nobody in there. Maybe I have the wrong address? I get the flyer out of my purse and read it again.

"Adults," says the flyer in big bolded letters, and then, a little smaller: "Practice your English in a relaxed setting." And after: "English Second Language Conversation Group. Join volunteer tutors for drop-in English conversation at the Canmore Legion. All language learners are welcome."

I am a language learner, and the sign hanging outside the door says, The Royal Canadian Legion, Branch #3 Three Sisters. But the place is empty.

I assume it's closed, and I'm ready to leave when a call from across the half-darkness convinces me to take a couple of steps inside. A woman walks briskly toward me. In front of her strident energy, the sleepy space opens up like the sea in front of Moses. "You're with the Conversation Group, aren't you?"

Yes, I am. It's my first time at the Legion, my first time meeting the group. "But you're very early, dear." It's like a beacon, her quick smile in the dim light. "We just opened. Sit down whenever you like. I will be back with a pot of coffee for all of you." And she disappears into a second room, behind a bar.

I am left alone on a vinyl chair.

My hand still clutches the flyer. I look at it again. A guy with a typically nondescript stock-photo face looks back at me. He's "the volunteer"; his expression looks neutral in an attentive kind of way. I think he looks uncomfortable, not sure of what's expected from him; a little lost. I can relate to that.

Or maybe I am just imagining things.

What kind of a place is this, anyway?

The Bow Valley is full of fancy restaurants and trendy little coffee shops. This is not one of them. Here, there is no mountain hipster vibe, no trees painted by local artists in Emily Carr's style; there are no feel-good messages written in chalk to be read by locals in sleek running clothes while they sip at their lattes, no tourists wearing colourful toques and loopy scarves. I have a feeling that someone asking for an organic, free-trade, gluten-free cupcake will be secretly met with a roll of the eyes from the bartender lady.

"A relaxed setting," says my flyer.

I try to relax, but there are flags around me and, if I learned anything from my Communist childhood, it's that you cannot really relax around flags; especially when they are placed next to official portraits.

And there are six of them on the wall, and Queen Elizabeth looks serene somewhere above my head.

"I salute thee, my beloved flag..." a childish voice, my own shaky voice from long ago, singsongs inside my head. My back stiffens, my chin lifts, my hand starts rising to my imaginary beret, in a salute.

I catch myself in time and lower my arm, but the aborted reflex brings back a memory.

I am around 10 years old, and I am part of an official parade dedicated to Our Beloved Leader. My whole town is participating. I didn't ask to be here. Nobody did. But it doesn't matter. This is a big show and everybody has a role to play.

All the students are dressed in Pioneer uniforms: white shirts with a red tie; wide plastic belts with Communist Romania's coat of arms on the big metal buckle; pleated black skirts and knee-long white socks for girls, black slacks for boys; the obligatory black, white or brown shoes – but then, it's not like we have much of a choice, the shoes available in the stores are rarely in a different colour.

The children in my school are instructed to form two long rows stretching on both sides of the street.

After, we are ordered to stand to attention. We are not allowed to talk among ourselves. The teachers' eyes dig into our backs, making sure we stay rooted on the designated spots and salute.

The exact position was to be strictly followed: the right arm at 90 degrees to the body, the bent elbow with the open palm facing forward, the fingertips not touching the forehead, just hovering in the corner of the right eye.

Behind us, there are adults – waving and clapping.

In front of us, the parade: red flags and official portraits of Our Beloved Leader, continuous streams running sluggishly down the streets, making their way toward the city square.

And we, the Pioneers, the "young Communists in the making," saluting.

It's a hot day and I am thirsty. After awhile, I feel the sweat running down the back of my neck, soaking my shirt. My arm hurts and starts shaking. I would like to lower it, but I know I am not allowed to. I just want this stupid parade to be over already. On top of everything else, I feel myself sinking. I dare to glance at my feet. To my dismay, I am standing on a melting puddle of tar. It's not deep, but the soles of my shoes are already encased in it. I try lifting my leg; my shoe doesn't budge. I am tired and thirsty and my arm hurts, and now I can't even move my feet. The thoughts in my head start running like crazy: "I'm stuck! I am stuck here! I can't leave!" In my mind flashes for a second the image of a lonely little girl, forever stuck to this spot, forced forever to salute an endless parade of red flags.

I panic, and in a flash I jump out of my tar-imprisoned shoes. I bolt, pushing my way through the crowd. I just want out of here.

If a teacher yelled after me, I didn't hear. On empty

side streets, I run all the way home as fast as my legs in white socks can carry me.

∧ ∧ ∧

Inside the Canmore Legion, my right arm aches from a pain from long ago. I stand, abruptly, trying to shake the vivid memory.

I go on to the other room, where the bar is. It's sunnier. I approach my Moses lady and I ask for a coffee. She brings some in a big cup and I want to pay for it, but she shrugs and smiles brightly, "Don't worry about it, dear; I didn't open the cash register yet. The milk and sugar are on that table." I smile back and sit down at a table, watching her going about, cleaning and carrying little boxes and bags, pushing chairs, moving bottles.

It dawns on me that she's not at all intimidated by those flags, official portraits and coats of arms, those sport trophies, military insignia and war paintings – all those things that almost made me leave.

She's running her everyday business, unperturbed, and I again turn my attention to around me, more inclined than before to understand this place instead of just dismissing it.

It's a strange mixture between a bar and a military museum, with a very manly flavour.

"The Canmore Legionnaires. 1951-2," reads a label under the picture of a serious-looking hockey team. There are a Lancaster and a Chalowski among them; a Whitehead and a Kriszan.

Young faces smile from another frame called "For

Valour. Commemorating the 16 Canadian Servicemen awarded the Victoria Cross for bravery during World War II."

On a different wall, a poster announces in beautiful handwritten letters: "The House Rules for 8-Ball." Rule number five says: "Either the cue ball or object ball must hit a rail to become a legal hook."

I have no idea what this means.

I understand the words but not the meaning. The same with the faces: I can identify the smiles or the frowns, but what's behind those soldiers' smiles I don't know; and I can read the names, but they don't mean anything to me.

All these objects displayed tell the story of a past I don't belong to. This is not my past. I can't relate to this pride. My past is somewhere in Europe, has parades and red flags. I walked away from it.

Both of my hands hold the cup of coffee; I feel its warmth seeping through. I wonder if someone could choose their own past.

Could I?

I am not that frightened little girl anymore. I refuse to let the past weigh me down. And I believe I could find in this new past so proudly displayed around me an episode I can relate to.

How hard can it be?

I'm suddenly determined. I am going to understand; maybe not the full story, but at least a small part of it. I am going to pick an object from this different past; I will understand its story, I will understand its meaning, I will make it mine.

The little enamel plaque under the painting (a copy, actually) in front of me summarizes the subject "Typhoon Fury. Belgium, 1944. Typhoon pilot Harry Hardy of 440 Squadron R.C.A.F. Overflies German Heavy Armour Position." The Second World War is a familiar story. My parents were both war children.

I spot the good guys. They are flying the planes with concentric circles on their wings so high that I can't really distinguish their faces. The planes are not the focus of the painting, though. My eyes are drawn to the tank engulfed in flames with a black cross on its side. These are the bad guys, I acknowledge. Good guys flying away, the tank stopped. End of story. I already feel more confident, stand taller. It was an easy one. I understand this story.

Except that I don't. There is a soldier on top of the turret, trying to pull another one out of the tank. He looks vulnerable standing up there, with no helmet, in the planes' direct sight. And there is another one, hiding in the shadow, holding in his arms a wounded or, more likely, dead comrade. You can clearly see his worried face turned toward the sky. Strangely, in the middle of the fight, there is a dog barking at the planes.

I wonder what happened to the dog. Did it survive? What about the soldier on top of the tank? Did he save the other? Did he save himself? All these bad guys, cowering, trying to save their wounded; worried, gunned down by a faceless man. Suddenly I'm annoyed with the painter. I wish the bad guys looked less human. Why do I have to witness their fear? It was supposed to be a simple story.

I lose my confidence again, the floor becomes less firm, I'm again a scuba diver in a sunken ship, casting my light this way and that, trying to understand what I see in my trembling flame, trying to make sense of those sand-covered shapes, of those blurred fallen silhouettes, to sort them out, to decide what deserves to be saved, what I can take back into the sun, or what should be left to sleep, undisturbed, in the deep.

PULLING UP STAKES

Rob Alexander

The field behind my childhood home in Canmore was small as far as fields go. It stretched less than a block long and only one lot in width, but it was filled with tall grass and gnarled white-barked trembling aspen with their rattling leaves. Coyotes often gathered in this field as night fell, announcing their arrival with high-pitched howls and yips that reverberated through the house, waking me and my sister Lesley, vaulting us from a dead sleep to a full-out run to our parents' room. We'd climb up onto my mom's hope chest, and with the smooth wood cold beneath our feet, we'd stare out the window into the night and watch the sleek and shadowy shapes entwine in a mass of bushy tails. Some nights, the coyotes stayed for a long time, playing and calling back and forth. On other nights, the coyotes melted back into the ragged black shadows of the nearby forest just as quickly as they had arrived, their echoing calls disappearing among the trees.

No matter how long the coyotes stayed, they always came back. It might be the next night, a few nights or perhaps a week, maybe even more, but they always returned. At least they did until the bulldozers rumbled into the field one day and scraped it clean. Once the field had been reduced to bare earth, loose rocks and wooden surveyor stakes tipped with orange tape, the coyotes vanished. And like Don Quixote charging windmills, Lesley and I walked the dead field yanking stakes in a vain attempt to bring back the grass, the aspens and the coyotes. What else can two children do in the face of progress?

After the bulldozer had done its work and the builders moved in, it was a rare night that we heard a long, plaintive cry in the darkness, and when we did, it was always off in the distance. I never gave any thought to what our house and Mount Peechee Place looked like before we lived there, however. In my mind, both had always been there, just like the field. I'm sure that before the bulldozers and excavators and builders began their work on what became my home, Canmore kids had been busy pulling stakes.

Canmore at that time was small, confined to the valley bottom. Split in half by the Bow River, it sat in a ring around the downtown core, and everything beyond the developed limits served as an extended playground. But every time a new road or subdivision began, myself and all of the other Canmore kids, just like the coyotes, were pushed from the places we knew, the places where we played, hiked, camped, built forts, climbed trees, wandered and roamed—the places where the land allowed us to be kids. Like the coyotes, we kept losing our fields and forests. Before I begin to sound like a fist-shaking curmudgeon yelling at kids to get off my lawn, I'm not against change; it's necessary, invigorating and can lead to good ideas and new opportunities (the new Canmore has given me many opportunities the old Canmore couldn't have), but change can also be difficult, even painful, especially when we have no say in the matter.

In his eloquent exploration of the American Southwest, *Landscape of Desire: Identity and Nature in Utah's Canyon Country*, Greg Gordon, an instructor at Dixie State University in St. George, Utah, believes that we are inclined to lament imposed change, as it removes us from the places we know and love. "When we've pinned our soul to a place," Gordon writes, "we resent imposed changes. They invalidate our memories, which cease to be living things and become consigned to the realm of ghosts. Such irreversible changes hurl us against our will from past to present tense." For some people, that's not a problem; they're happy in the present. But for others, such as myself, the past is where we tend to dwell—it's the difference between optimism versus pessimism.

Lesley, the optimist, was able to keep a firm eye on what she loved about Canmore and why this place was important to her. She was at ease with the imposed changes—the loss of the quiet places we knew and loved and the shift toward a busy high-end resort—for they did not invalidate her memories, and as a result, she never strayed far. And me, the overly sentimental pessimist who lives in the past? I always had difficulty accepting the way Canmore has gone, the way my memories have been invalidated.

My childhood was idyllic, spent outdoors in the nearby forest and along the Bow River. My experience as a youth and teenager in Canmore was not. I have a profound learning disability that went undiagnosed until I went to see an educational psychologist shortly after I turned 30 years old. Unable to learn even the simplest technical concepts kids, parents and teachers take for granted—simple multiplication, greater than/less than or even grammar—how I saw the world eroded away until the only filter I had left to view the world was clouded by a haze of depression and anxiety. With no understanding of who I was or what I was experiencing, I blamed Canmore. Not the most rational or healthy idea, but my learning disability, and the subsequent depression and anxiety that came with it, invalidated all that I knew as positive about Canmore; all that I loved had been tainted. The physical changes came to stand in as a proxy for the emotional, psychological changes.

I left Canmore in 1989, returning each summer to work for Parks Canada as a campground attendant, but it would be ten years before I felt it was time to come home as a full-time resident. I wanted to confront my ghosts, and I managed to create a happy relationship with my town, despite how it has changed. It's one thing to come to terms with imposed physical changes; it's another thing altogether to accept the most unwelcome of imposed changes: death.

Lesley began complaining in the spring of 2013 of being unable to eat. Everything made her feel sick. She also had headaches, but that was nothing new. She had suffered from migraines for many years, a result of having scoliosis as a child. Her spine and jaw were bent, a little crooked, not unlike her sense of the world (as I would remind her regularly). And despite corrective surgery, the migraines were a regular part of her life. She finally was admitted into the Canmore Hospital for tests and observation, and then a few days later she was transferred to the Tom Baker Cancer Centre at the Foothills Hospital, where it was discovered that she had an aggressive Stage 4 cancer that had riddled her body with tumours. Lungs. Organs. Brain. The doctors tried radiation on her brain in the hope of shrinking the tumours, but with no success. Lesley died Friday, August 9, 2013, at the age of 46.

And in the irrational way that I blamed Canmore's physical changes as a proxy for my anger at the way my learning disability pulled me apart, I did it again after Lesley died. Everywhere I turned I saw her, but not in a happy way. Even today, three years out, the image of her stricken with cancer – impossibly thin, sunken eyes, bald head, her slim hands wrapped around the railings to ground herself and ward off the nausea – is all I see.

I came to see paradise as heartless and cruel. And while still living in Canmore, I could get no distance, find no space to breathe. As luck or good timing would have it, I have some distance now. Living an hour away in Calgary, I can see that my love for my mountain home was being replaced with bitterness and anger. My soul is still pinned to Canmore, but pins, while they serve to hold us in place, are sharp and can hurt. And when I'm stabbed with a pin, I pull it out. It's the same with Canmore: it hurt to be there, so I had to pull the pin out, and rather than letting the pin slip free altogether, what I needed most was a change.

And when people inevitably ask me if I miss Canmore and I say, "No, not really," I'm only giving them part of the truth. I do miss Canmore, but at least, as Gordon reminds me in his book, my memories can continue to be living things and not consigned to the realm of ghosts. I can keep from being hurled against my will into the present tense and remain in the past tense, where I can see Lesley and Canmore as both were before cancer. For now, paradise is better just beyond the horizon.

THREE VALLEYS

Frances Klatzel

It is those early morning sounds that creep into my consciousness as I wake to remind myself which valley I'm awakening in today.

These sounds symbolize very different places, spread over the geography of half the world.

The sound of the train whistles echoing in the Bow Valley echo from my childhood memories: a sound of security and a sense of place. The train whistles going up and down the Bow River Valley create a sense of connectedness – running through generations of lives in my mother's family, from grassy ravines where my grandparents grazed horses and cattle. At the headwaters as a younger woman, I explored the glaciers in the Rockies. Train whistles – a sound of progress, movement, connections on the long ribbon of steel to the outside world.

More early morning sounds: the clinking and clanking of yak bells in the valley below Mount Everest.

Mountain scenery first attracted me to the Himalaya, but the warm, friendly people became my enduring connection. From 1983 to 1989, I had the opportunity and privilege to live and work with Sherpa people in the Khumbu Valley of east Nepal, near Mount Everest, helping to create a museum of Sherpa culture at Tengboche Monastery. The Sherpas are renowned through the literature of adventure, where they have earned an international reputation for their work on mountaineering expeditions, especially on Everest. However, this reputation focuses on an occupation, rather than the Sherpas' rich cultural heritage.

Being blessed with communities of friends and family on two sides of the world, it has been almost 33 years since I first came to Nepal. Not all of that time has been spent here, so I am still strongly connected to my roots in Canada, all along the Bow River from its source in the mountains to its gorge through the southern Alberta ranchlands.

But certainly many family and friends in Canada wonder what is the pull of Nepal, what keeps me half a world away.

The Bow Valley and Khumbu Valley are both almost iconic mountain valleys, both World Heritage Sites, both on trade or transportation routes. But with key differences.

Khumbu is inhabited by the indigenous Sherpa ethnic group, which sometimes struggles to maintain control of its valley. Ironically, I know more about the Sherpa indigenous perception of the land than I do about the Stoney perception of the Bow Valley, where my great-grandfather (mother's side) came and settled near Calgary over 130 years ago.

In the Khumbu Valley, the Sherpa ethnic people came over the Himalaya fleeing unrest in Tibet. On the shoulders of these mountains, they grew buckwheat and barley and grazed yaks for milk and wool. For centuries, the Sherpa supplemented this subsistence agriculture by trading goods with Tibetans over the pass on the crest of the Himalaya. When that trade became more difficult, Sherpas were fortunate that a mountain at the head of the valley was found to be the highest point on Earth.

Tourism and mountaineering brought new livelihoods to the Sherpas as they carried loads on the rocky trails and over the glaciated peaks, often at great risk to their own lives. I often laugh at how we relate to the Sherpas, since the Bow Valley has also come to survive on tourism.

In the 1980s, Khumbu's tenuous link to the outside world was a young man hired to run across the hills for a week to take mail back and forth to Kathmandu. Now, Internet and wireless allow instant communications from all but the very highest altitudes. In the 30 years I have spent time in Khumbu, I have seen the development and change that my grandparents saw in the Bow Valley over the 20th century.

In Canada, I worked in the national parks, where the reasons for conservation are much more tied to preserving the landscape and forests for their own intrinsic value. This is a much more abstract rationale for conservation than the compelling reasons I found in Nepal, where indigenous people in the area depend on the forests for their survival.

The museum described mostly what the abbot of Tengboche calls the Sherpas' "inner culture" and the importance of ceremonies that link their spiritual and physical lives. The preparation of the museum took time because it was essential to first know the people and the many dimensions of their culture in order to accurately and concisely depict it.

While compiling information for the museum, I often found that conversations encompassed aspects of philosophy, psychology and spirituality. Often the subjects we discussed wandered to the questions we seek to answer with religion or science: How did the earth begin? What happens after death? What is our relationship to nature? To our symbols in the environment?

Over the years, my questions turned from the intellectual to the intuitive. I began to experience the culture rather than question it. Life with the Sherpas revealed different ways of seeing the world. It peeled away my preconceived notions so that I began to appreciate the significance of rituals, traditions and symbols. In the process, I was changed.

Sherpa friends introduced me to a new way of seeing the world through everyday life. Whether monk or shepherd, they know who they are and what they believe as "Sherpa people."

Living in another culture forced me to think about how it works, to confront the ironies and inconsistencies of a different way of being. Soon, I realized that one layer of meaning reveals more queries within. The more one starts to understand, the more one realizes all there is to question and explore.

Just as working with the Sherpas opened my eyes to another way of perceiving the world, the conversations with these people helped me to understand the more difficult side of Nepal. They helped me to see both the sacred and the profane and start to understand and question world events in this era of intense politics and crisis. I have come to see that while outside cultures divide us, inner cultures, the core of all religions and beliefs, can bring us together.

Looking at other cultures as different from our own, we split the whole into parts. We analyze what we see happening and ask why. For people of the other culture, it is their way of life. We examine the oddity of different traditions and customs rather than the inner purposes that might bring us into an understanding of the culture. We end up looking at how the "other" culture is different from ours rather than at our commonness in the wholeness of humankind.

Living in Nepal and doing documentation work for development projects in more recent years has offered me opportunities to talk with so many people in difficult circumstances – former bonded labourers, so-called untouchables, Hindu widows and farmers without enough fields to feed their families. I came to realize how the systems of hierarchy went beyond discrimination to actually keep some people poor.

Ultimately, we can build bridges of understanding between cultures in the world if we are not afraid just because they are different.

Over the years, I was moved by what I saw and experienced another way of being. I became a believer in the value of culture, not just outside culture but inside culture that manifests itself in everything we do, in what we say and think and how we say it. Culture becomes small actions in everyday life; it becomes our interactions with everyone we meet and touch in our lives. It becomes our relationship with ourselves and with nature.

I saw outside myself being with the Sherpas; I saw another way of existing with one another and with the world. I saw an acceptance of mystery and the questions we just can't answer for sure. I came back with a pair of eyeglasses, spectacles with which to look at myself and my culture with new eyes.

Tengboche Rinpoche, who I worked for on the Sherpa Cultural Centre for seven years, always talked about the coming "Kali Yuga," the age of crisis. At times he said that it would come in our lifetimes, and a few times told me that it would be better to be back in my own country. Eventually, he seemed to think that it was not going to matter where one was. Perhaps he thought that Nepal would be a microcosm of the world. Sometimes I did not want to listen when he talked about the Kali Yuga. It did not seem like something that would affect my life. Yet somehow I felt that someday Nepal would go through an intense time of conflict that would tear it apart. That time has come.

Rinpoche often said that we cannot continue to ignore other people's problems. It seems that this is so true for not just the Sherpas but also the more fortunate people in Nepal and in the world. In the old idyllic Nepal, it was possible to embrace the sacred and avoid the profane. It took almost ten years to get me to realize that we must also embrace the profane and not ignore the problems and difficulties of such a vast majority of the people in the world.

Why did I stay in a country during a civil war and now the aftermath of a huge earthquake? Just as one embraces one's friends in the good times and sticks by them in the bad, we must also embrace the sacred that Nepal has awakened in all of us and try to learn from the profane. We cannot go back to the idyllic Nepal we once knew with the discrimination and inequity that people just accepted.

I suppose that my first eight years in Nepal was more of an experience of the sacred. I met lamas, went on a pilgrimage and was filled with the wonder of exploring a new culture and starting to see the world through a new set of spectacles. I enriched my life beyond belief, even though it set me off on a rather unusual "career path." It might be the edges of the sacred and the profane – where both the awe-inspiring and the distressing experiences take me to new levels of wondering and questioning.

NOTHING TO DO IN THE BOW VALLEY

Carol Picard

Often in my life I have pitied the poor Bow Valley adolescent ... especially after I found one living in my basement.

Because apparently there is nothing to do around here.

Forget the mountains and their slopes, the hiking/biking/skiing trails, the indoor rinks and climbing walls, the epic golf courses and the amazing Banff Centre, the plethora of dance and gymnastics classes, the competitive swim clubs ... *there's nothing to do!!!!*

The universal lament of teens the world over, but I say this in all seriousness, having found my resident teen as out of place here as a captive parrot or a relocated bear. For many of us valley parents, we are raising our children far away from their native habitat, forcing them to come of age in a world precariously close to the wilderness.

With no ready access to cacophonous consumer temples, their subconscious has instead been force-fed the silence of spruce forests and overhead galaxies in inky skies. The smell of wood smoke and wolf willow fills their nostrils and the *k-k-k-krak* of the omnipresent raven their ears.

We drill into them the need to carry bear spray and we educate them in avalanche conditions and extrication. They learn to identify and assess animal scat and footprints to know what else is walking their path. High-school food courses include foraging for edibles in the surrounding undergrowth.

In the greater journey of life, this will serve them well and they will look back with the kind of affectionate nostalgia every childhood deserves.

In the immediacy of adolescence, though, if their heart yearns for the bright lights of the big city and its endless à la carte options of movies, theatre, dance, shopping and music – well, it's not quite hell, but it is certainly purgatory.

And it is, of course, all our fault.

We as adults find ourselves here for a variety of reasons. We have come because we have a need to challenge ourselves to extremes, economically, artistically or athletically. For some, life's circumstances have washed us up on these shores. For a scant few, we were actually born and raised here and have chosen to stay.

Our offspring have no such choice. They're here because the parental units are here.

They are raised in an ethos of ambition that permeates their lives from the womb. In a world where parenting has become a competitive sport, Bow Valley parents are on the podium.

Valley communities are a cesspool of success, with Olympians and Everest veterans on every street corner, and more published authors, world-class photographers and visual artists per capita than Toronto. Occasionally we are joined by Supreme Court justices and former premiers; corporate CEOs whose stock options could buy most of Banff Avenue; and actors and musicians who could buy the CEOs. We are also ground zero for the now-defunct Temporary Foreign Worker program, a program that fed our voracious need for front-line hospitality industry workers. A decade after its inception, many of those newcomers have permanent residency and are reunited with the teens that were mere babies when the parents left for Canada.

We spend more on their bikes and skis than we do on their food, and we introduce them to rock climbing and steep, single-track bike trails before they hit kindergarten. By 12 they've been exposed to soccer, baseball, hiking, ice climbing, competitive gymnastics, competitive swimming, competitive dance, downhill and cross-country skiing, snowboarding and unicycling.

In some kids this immersion parenting fosters a lifelong passion for sports and the outdoors. In others ... not so much. Somewhere along that path, some parents are forced to confront the reality – this kid is just not into the mountains. Or the outdoors. Or fresh, pine-scented air.

No, what they're into is live alternative music and transcendent philosophy. Vans Warped Tour and Folk

Alliance International. The elk in the front yard elicit a mild "Oh, neat," and a suggestion of a seven a.m. departure for a day at Sunshine is met with a stony glare.

They come of age in a very small fishbowl, and if you're the neon tetra in a school full of guppies, you're either completely standing out in the crowd or lurking in the little plastic castle at the bottom of the tank. The world of haves and have-nots, popular or unpopular, is in our kids' faces on a daily basis, and the confusion, angst and self-searching that define adolescence take place here in a tiny cohort that magnifies and distorts one's relative place in the world.

That fishbowl limits their opportunities for free-range mischief and vandalism, under constant scrutiny from parents, teachers, friends of parents and friends' parents. Underage drinking in the local bars is nigh on impossible where everybody knows your name – or your folks.

Even their subversive activities are under the microscope. Not a house party can be held without the whole town knowing. In Canmore, the rite of passage is the venerable bush party at the QC, a clearing on a quasi-island in the Bow where the youth of the community have been partying for six generations. Well known to the local RCMP, it's monitored on a regular basis.

Sounds like paradise? Parents might think so, but our offspring are pretty desperate to leave. Come graduation, there's a stampede of young boots hitting the highways and airports to get the heck out of here and make their mark upon the world at large.

Some, those who have embraced the mountain

lifestyle in which they've been steeped, dive deeper into the experience, heading off to Revelstoke or Golden to train as mountain guides or work as lifties at a less familiar ski resort where everybody doesn't know your name.

Those on the post-secondary path take out monstrous student loans and scatter across the country to Vancouver, Montreal, Toronto and beyond, their parents dropping them off with worried glances at the marijuana dispensary two doors down from the new apartment, wondering aloud whether they've remembered their bear spray.

And then the parents come home to watch the ironic influx of hundreds of other people's children, stampeding to the valley to ski, climb, hike, bike and revel in the wilderness experience of these small mountain towns where, soon, everybody does know their name. And, maybe, along with adventure, that's what they were looking for.

A LETTER FROM THE BOW VALLEY

Michale Lang

Dearest Friend,

Finally, I have reached the seventh anniversary of my return to Banff. Before I moved here, only my closest friends knew how I longed to live in the mountains again, even though I am neither an adventurer nor a climber. As you know, I am more bookish than bold.

You will remember that I have always enjoyed reading letters from the past. Letters written by soldiers to their loved ones at home have particularly touched me. But the long letters written by Catharine Whyte to her family and friends in the United States have also inspired me. With the introduction of emails, texts and social media to the current generations, don't you worry that the art of letter writing seems to be an endangered species? I still enjoy writing letters to you and a few other close friends.

Please bear with me while I reminisce about some of our times together and remind myself why I moved back here.

After we met in the '70s at Lake O'Hara, where I worked, you used to visit me each year for 13 years in Field, that small British Columbia railway town that was my home. It was a perpetual party then. You would stay for a few days on your way in or out of the backcountry, and we would talk about our lives over the past 12 months and play music late into the night. My friendships from that time are still amongst my strongest connections.

In those days, the Great Divide was no barrier. When we were young, we would hitchhike to Banff to buy groceries every two weeks when we got paid. Compared to Field, Banff felt like a city. It had shops, a movie theatre, and even in the early '70s, it had some good restaurants and places to go dancing. We always loved dancing. Do you remember those days, the '70s and '80s? Silver City was hopping then, and Giorgio's and Le Beaujolais were great places to eat on special occasions if we could afford it. There were the concerts at the Banff Centre; a bunch of us would hop in somebody's car and drive in together to see a concert and then drive home late at night, often in blinding snowstorms. But the weather never stopped us, because we were young and had no concept of our own mortality.

In fact, the cultural attraction of the Banff Centre partially influenced our decision to live in Banff. Before moving here, you may recall, I had been a poetry student for a short time at the centre and had come to appreciate its role in developing the arts in Canada. But the primary draw was the mountains. When I left Field for the city in the mid-'80s, I would yearn for the mountains. Living in Calgary near the university, I could see a small slice of mountains from my high-rise apartment. I would stand in that window and mourn the loss of my home, even though it had been my choice to leave.

As you know, I first left the mountains to get an education, to pursue a career, but the mountains had gotten hold of me. The Rockies were in my blood and bones and I knew I couldn't stay away forever. Every weekend was spent driving to the mountains for cross-country skiing in winter and hiking in summer, but it was never enough. Although Calgarians (and I was one of them for 19 years) think that the Rockies are their backyard, living in the city does not compare to living here in the shadow of the mountains. But you know that.

I finished university, went up north to Lac La Biche to work, did a master's degree, worked and worked, bought a house, did another degree, and worked my way up from programmer to executive director in museums small and large. I gained experience and I bided my time until, finally, after more than 20 years working all over Alberta, an opening came up at the Whyte Museum of the Canadian Rockies. It was a golden opportunity. As executive director and curator, I was able to explore not only the community's present but its rich and diverse past. Curating *Gateway to the Rockies*, an exhibit about the history of this area, I learned and grew. I befriended pioneers like Ralphine Locke and Stoney Elders like Bill McLean, Walking Buffalo's son. And not only was I able to explore the history through first-hand accounts, images and books of the people who made this place what it is today but I walked and rode and canoed the landscape of that history. I pushed myself beyond my comfort level to gain a sense of their experience so that I could better tell their stories.

Do you remember when we paddled across Alberta in a voyageur canoe with that brigade celebrating the David Thompson bicentennial? More than 200 canoeists from all over the world, and some of them canoed 3700 kilometres, all the way from Rocky Mountain House to Fort William in Ontario! It was a taste of what the early explorers of this area experienced. And, of course, there was that crazy horse-packing trip that we took to gain first-hand experience of what it was like for Mary Schäffer (my favourite early 20th-century photographer) and others to travel through the mountains on horseback. Or do you remember me telling you about our hikes with a retired warden in the northeast end of Banff National Park, where the bison roamed and where they will soon return? The first was along the Red Deer River, beginning at the beautiful Ya Ha Tinda Ranch on Banff Park's eastern slope. On another trip, we had to cross the raging Panther River with water swirling to our waists. But it was worth it to stay in those wardens' cabins, especially Windy Cabin, that I had heard so much about from wardens' wives like Irene Brook and Dorothy Carleton. Dorothy is the dear war bride, who came from England in the '40s to join her warden husband at Bow Summit and, who, in her 90s, still leads the seniors' choir. I am sure you remember her from my mother's funeral. She really is unforgettable. You would certainly remember my friend Irene. Did I ever tell you that she studied at the Banff Centre with the Group of Seven in the 1940s? Her husband, Glen, was a warden in Kootenay and Yoho national parks. She first came to Banff from northern Saskatchewan to study art when the Banff Centre was in its infancy. She told me stories of these old curmudgeons who taught her, one of whom happened to be A.Y. Jackson. She later returned to work at the Bay in Banff and met her warden husband soon after he returned from the Second World War. At that time, the wardens had to ski out to the trains in winter to get to town because the roads were only open in summer. Their wives and families lived with them in back-country cabins and had little contact with the outside world for months at a time.

With you, we explored the areas where Peter and Catharine Whyte painted. Their art is such a legacy. Wasn't it fascinating to stand where they painted and see how much the landscape has changed – how the glaciers have receded and the trees have grown taller? It is always great to meet you at Skoki, where Peter and Catharine helped build that amazing backcountry lodge. Hiking into Mount Assiniboine at least once every year reminds me of the stories of Erling Strom and the climbers who first conquered that incredible peak. Do you remember when we met there in early September and there was more than a foot of snow? Hiking out through the old route over Allenby Pass and along Brewster Creek was such an amazing experience! As we emerged onto the craziness of Banff Avenue in midsummer after days in the backcountry, it was surreal.

But it is the everyday life here that I cherish most, moments like walking home from work with a wolf watching me from the hill above the road. He followed me all the way home to satisfy his curiosity. I never felt the least bit threatened. Or the morning at Vermilion Lakes when the wolf pack ran by, their paws thrumming the earth as they swiftly passed. Seeing elk or deer almost daily, or occasionally encountering a bear on a walk near town, is the most remarkable thing. It is easy to accept having wildlife in our backyard as commonplace, but where else in the world is this possible? Perhaps in the far north or other remote places, but there, the wildlife is game. Here, they are protected.

You have often asked me what it is like to live in a place with so many tourists. It seldom bothers me. We work around it. In the peak seasons, we do our grocery shopping in the early morning or late evening. We walk instead of driving to avoid having to park in the overcrowded townsite. We keep in mind that these tourists are the livelihood of most people who live here. And it is wonderful to meet people from around the world. I do not mind answering their questions, because they help me to see this place with fresh eyes, to remember that it truly is special. And, of course, I have met some of my closest friends, including you and my husband, through chance encounters with tourists, as you both were when I met you.

It is also those tourists who help support the services that make Banff such a great place to live, and not just restaurants, coffee shops or fudgeries. I am grateful to have the best hospital in Alberta here in our town and another hospital with excellent services in our neighbouring community of Canmore. You know that my mother had the best care here in her final days with sensitive and compassionate doctors and nurses providing support for all of us. No one could hope for more.

In your last letter, you asked me about my plans for the future. Well, this is it. I am content here. I have lived and worked from one end of Alberta to the other and even strayed into BC. But this is where I want to settle. Like Mary Schäffer, I plan to "Tarry a While" (do you remember that is what she named her house in Banff?). My work still takes me away from time to time and I enjoy the unique culture and history of other places (even Fort McMurray), but it is always good to come home. Like you, I love to travel, but my heart lies in the Rockies. Although it is not always an easy place to live, with snow and ice, bitter winds and tourists, I hope to reside in the Bow Valley until I die. When I am too old to hike or ski, all I ask is that, like my mother, I can look out the window at the mountains and occasionally see a passing deer or a soaring raven.

I think I will exhaust your patience if I continue to rave about my home in the Bow Valley. I look forward to your visit this summer and our soak in the Sulphur Mountain hot springs. All the best until we meet again in the mountains.

Sincerely, Michale

PART THREE

The Politics of Place

BANFF NATIONAL PARK

ALWAYS A WORLD
HERITAGE SITE

Harvey Locke

Banff National Park belongs to everyone. It even belongs to those yet unborn. Ours to love but not to exploit, Banff is known around the world for its natural magnificence. Less well known is the park's deep human history. Throughout the long presence of people in North America it has been a travel corridor and a place where people have stayed. It has seen the passage of many cultures but never been the exclusive territory of anyone. In that sense, it has been a world heritage site for over 10,000 years.

Millions of people feel a strong connection to this place. Here is mine. It arises from my love of the landscape and the things that live here and from my family's deep roots in the area. From my house in Banff I can walk to the Banff Cemetery and visit both my great-grandparent Locke's graves. I can cross-country ski to Brewster Creek, which is named after another great-grandparent, I can hike over Harvey Pass, which is named for my grandfather, or I can admire Locke's Schuss, the cliff behind the Sunshine Inn, which is named for my father, who skied it first. The ashes of mother, Ralphine, who was the first person we know of to have been born at Lake Louise, and those of her mother and her two sisters are also in Banff. If I go down the valley to Morley, I can visit the graves of my great-great-grandparents Boyd, who joined their Mc-Dougall cousins at Morleyville to create the first Euro-Canadian community in southern Alberta. Yet my family's six generations here are but a thin slice of the deep human history in this globally cherished and shared landscape. It is a story that spans 500 generations.

In historical times, Banff was a place used by many different Aboriginal cultures. Before the railway came through, my great-grandfather James Irvine Brewster visited the area where the town of Banff is now located and observed an Indian burial platform in some poplar trees. The hot springs on Sulphur Mountain were visited by Aboriginal people of many cultures, some of whom were traditional enemies, such as the Blackfoot and Stoney. But the hot springs were a place of peace where enemies downed their weapons so all could partake of the magical waters.

The diverse array of Aboriginal cultures that have

known this valley intimately is reflected in the names of the mountains around Banff. Stoney Squaw Mountain stands north of town. Mount Peechee, in the Fairholme Range east of town, is named for Cree guide Piché, who led Hudson's Bay Company Director Sir George Simpson through the Bow Valley in 1841 on the first trip around the world by land. When that party was in Fort Edmonton, they encountered another early visitor, the Methodist missionary Rev. Robert Rundle. Piché gave Rundle a sketch map of the Banff region, which is the earliest detailed sketch known to have been made of what would become Banff National Park.

Rundle roamed the landscape east of the Rockies and into the mountains in search of souls for several years. He came to the Banff townsite area in June 1847, where he encountered Assiniboine people (Stoney or Nakoda Sioux) in a camp west of Lake Minnewanka. Rundle's journal entries give a sense of the vast variety of Aboriginal cultures that were in southern Alberta in historic times. Three weeks before his visit to Banff, he was camped with Aboriginal people near the Highwood River in what is now southern Alberta and recorded some oral history: "June 5 Sat *Mem*. About 50 or 60 years hence Battle was fought just here between Peagans, Blood Indians, Blackfeet & Crees, Sucees (also two or 3 Ass. Strongwood). Other side there were Kootanies, Flat heads, Nez Perces, Snakes and Crow Indians, at least 500 hundred on each side (by accounts)." By way of explanation, "Sucees" refers to Sarcees or Tsuu T'ina (a Dene-speaking people) and "Ass." refers to Assiniboines. The usual division of alliances on the northern plains was Blackfoot and Tsuu T'ina on one side and Assiniboine and Cree on the other. It seems they joined forces for this great battle on the principle that the enemy of my enemy is my friend.

Howse Pass, in what is now the north end of Banff Park, was used by Ktunaxa people (anglicized to Kootenay). They travelled from the dry Columbia Valley through what are now Yoho and Kootenay parks and over Howse Pass to the Kootenay Plains and beyond in search of buffalo. In 1807 fur trader and mapmaker David Thompson first crossed Howse Pass by the old Ktunaxa route. After a few years of use, fur trader passage was barred in 1810 by a group of Peigan (Blackfoot Confederacy) warriors who were camping near its east portal.

Thompson was in this part of the world on several different occasions in the late 1700s and early 1800s. He noted that in his day the plains belonged to the Stone Indians (Assiniboine) and their strict allies the Nathaways (Cree), the Atsina, and the Peigan, Blood and Siksika tribes of the Blackfoot Confederacy. When he spent the winter of 1787–88 in the lodge of Young Man (Saukamappee), a Cree who lived among the Peigan in southern Alberta, the oral history of how that came to be was explained to him. Around 1730 the Peigan were a frontier tribe. They, with Cree support, displaced the Kootenay to the north, the Salish in the middle and the Snake Indians to the south, all of whom took refuge across the mountains. This broadly coincides with the history Rundle was told, though the dates differ, which doesn't matter much with oral history.

Where the oral histories of people with pre-European associations with Banff National Park taper off, archaeological evidence takes over. There are pit house depressions in several areas near Banff townsite and in the park's Red Deer River Valley. These are complex living sites where a number of past activities can be determined from the remains. Parks Canada archaeologist Gwyn Langemann determined that these pit houses and associated cultural traces correspond to the styles of Salish people of the Interior Plateau of British Columbia. They came and hunted for meat – buffalo bones are found in their firepits. These pit dwellings span an enormous time frame, from 440 Before Present to 2800 BP.

Archaeological digs done near Vermilion Lakes and Clovis points found near Lake Minnewanka take us even further back in time, even to the very first humans known in North America. The Vermilion Lakes site contained evidence of 11 different cultures spanning many thousand years. The oldest site predates 10,800 years BP. The dig was done from 1983 to 1985, at a time when the Clovis culture was thought to be the very first in North America. Clovis and Folsom (another culture that followed Clovis) points had been found near Lake Minnewanka, but the first layer at Vermilion Lakes contained artifacts that were different and older. In a 1995 paper, Parks Canada archaeologist Daryl Fedje and co-authors wrote that these earliest remains could not be assigned to a known cultural group. By 2015, Clovis were no longer considered the first North Americans, and an earlier mobile hunter-gatherer society was recognized as the precursor culture to the more sedentary Clovis.

To whom, then, does Banff National Park belong historically? The answer is clear: to no one in particular and to everyone. Today, as it should be, that same pattern of shared ownership is reflected in a national law and in international treaty.

Under the Canada National Parks Act, the park is dedicated to all Canadians to be enjoyed in a manner that leaves it unimpaired for future generations. I may live and have deep roots here, but that does not give me a superior claim to the park over any other Canadian. And through Banff National Park being part of the Canadian Rockies World Heritage Site, under the World Heritage Convention Canada has agreed that the park is a place of outstanding universal value to all people of the world. Through that treaty, Canada has further agreed to protect, conserve, present and transmit the park to future generations of all of humanity. Not only that, the responsibility to protect Banff National Park falls to more than just the people of Canada. The World Heritage Convention creates a duty on the entire international community to protect this special place.

Banff National Park has become an icon of Canada in the world and a proud part of Canadians' self-image. People come here from the far reaches of the earth to experience the magnificence of this shared treasure. On a sunny summer afternoon on the shore of Lake Louise you can observe every shape and form of human and hear a Babel of languages used to express awe in a hundred ways. That is just how it should be. Banff National Park belongs to us all. It always has.

THE HISTORY OF A FANTASY

Katherine Govier

When Rocky Mountains Park was created in 1887, this beautiful part of the world was deemed empty.

"The Indians seem to have feared and avoided the mountains," wrote Mabel Williams, the federal civil servant whose rhapsodic guidebooks emerged under the guidance of J.B. Harkin, former journalist and popular first parks commissioner. Mabel Williams was, of course, saying what she wished to be true. She was dead wrong, like others of her day.

Williams is a story in herself, one of a surprising number of mid-life women who in the early years of the 20th century found new meaning for their lives in what is now Banff National Park. Others include the American Quakers Mary Vaux and Mary Schäffer, the runaway aristocrat Catharine Whyte of Boston, back-country lodge host Lizzie Rummel of Germany and the little-known but fascinating Welsh dowager Mary de la Beche Nicholl – who at 65, in 1904, hired mountain guide Jimmy Simpson to help her catch butterflies at Mount Assiniboine.

There are a hundred stories like that, about men and women transforming their lives. Wonderful stories, many of them scarcely known. Even the best known are tucked away in archives and out-of-print books; the rest are lost or the stuff of local lore. Pioneers still in living memory are being pushed offstage, their traces removed. They have gone out of fashion. The current version of Rocky Mountain National Park does not include them. They clutter up the wilderness and get in the way of the animals and give people the idea that humans, long ago, in the middle distance and even now, had a role here in the wilds.

The Rocky Mountains are essential to our image of ourselves as Canadians, and to Canada's image around the world. Yes, the long angle of Rundle, the stalwart Cascade, are immutable, and so, one imagines, would be the image we promulgate. But no. We tinker with it. We change it every few decades to suit the fashion. Poolside movie stars and bears eating out of car windows are passé. So now are outfitters, climbers, hikers: almost all the human stories are out of the picture. Now the top image is the profile of a majestic grizzly. It's no accident. The mountain parks are managed, like a kingdom, but the managers are no longer distant Ottawa bureaucrats. They are us. This is what we want to say: this untouched place is where animals roam.

But what if we, like Mabel Williams, are deluded? What if we are in the grip of a fantasy?

A century and more ago, the idea of empty mountains

was inviting, seductive and, most of all, *convenient* for the dreamers. The Rocky Mountains comprised to them a brilliant kingdom reserved for human pleasure, offering relief from the workaday world. It was to be ruled invisibly by men in suits. But it was known intimately only by the "inconvenient" Natives, as Tom King has so profoundly named them, and the not-much-welcome trappers, settlers, shopkeepers and miners who called the mountains home.

People like Tom Wilson, born in Bond Head, Ontario, near Barrie. He went west at 18 and joined the NWMP at Fort Walsh in 1880, but quit when he became convinced the government was deliberately starving the Indians. He moved on to Banff. Wilson showed the CPR where they should build the Banff Springs Hotel. He guided the sclerotic Colonel Rogers over the pass that bears his name. "Give Rogers six plugs of chewing tobacco and five bacon rinds and he'll travel for two weeks." By Wilson's account, Rogers made his trail over the Rockies by killing trees with tobacco juice: "Not many trees along the trail escaped his deadly aim." Like most of these early guides, Wilson had a good sense of humour and made light of the difficulties. "I never knew how hard a time we had until I read the book," he said later.

Wilson is said to have been the first white man to see Lake Louise. He was certainly among the very few to witness the trumpeter swans that landed there before human activity drove them to more remote lakes. He worked with Native guides, including the "Twin" brothers, Joshua and William. He guided, among many others, the novelist Agnes Laut to Nigel Pass. Her first novel, *Lords of the North*, and many later books drew on her summers in the Rockies. But there is no biography of Tom Wilson. His particular style of pinched felt hat is memorialized with the words "Trail Blazer" in the Banff Cemetery.

Nor is there much public information about Arthur O. Wheeler, the land surveyor who founded the Alpine Club of Canada with *Winnipeg Free Press* reporter Elizabeth Parker in 1906. Unlike its US counterpart, the Alpine Club of Canada always had women members – in *Pushing the Limits: The Story of Canadian Mountaineering*, Chic Scott describes "ladies with long skirts and straw hats decorated with flowers" – as well as "men with derby hats and summer straws, some carrying umbrellas." Stirring prose marked Parker's contributions to the club: she tells us that "traversing the sources of the great ice rivers and breathing the virgin air above their mute snows is conducive to [a] philosophic [state of] mind." And while we're on climbers, what do we know of Edward Wheeler, Arthur's son, himself a climber and credited with showing Mallory the best route up Everest (a gesture that Mallory resented for the rest of his life)...?

More inclined to the public eye was Jimmy Simpson, a miscreant teenage poacher who arrived from Lincolnshire in 1896. He learned the ropes from his idol, Bill Peyto, a wild man who once carried a lynx into a bar on Banff Avenue. Simpson put a bit of capital he'd inherited into pack horses and for the next few decades led big-game hunters, American industrialists, atomic scientists and others on wide-ranging excursions through the Rockies. He laid out the route of the Banff–Jasper highway, and in his 60s travelled with zoologist Ian McTaggart-Cowan, sharing his knowledge of bighorn sheep. Simpson built Num-Ti-Jah Lodge. His fraught relationship with Parks management fills volumes at the Whyte Museum of the Canadian Rockies.

Intensely physical and practical, Simpson was nevertheless susceptible to mystical experience. "I went out in a cabin at the head of the Alexandra River ... It was a beautiful winter night, nice and warm. I was thinking what a beautiful country it was. I heard music orchestration came out of the southwest. It passed right over me, I heard it die away going to the NE. That was before radio or anything. It was not supposition or anything like that. I could hear the violins. There are so many amazing things in the world we don't know anything about."

That's an almost perfect expression of the popular 19th-century European notion of the sublime – spiritual transformation before the grandeur and pitilessness of nature. From the time the last spike was driven, CPR trains rolled west across the prairie, filled with the heartsick, the disillusioned, the pent-up, the extraneous and the man on the make. The dream brought mountaineers such as Edward Whymper, greatly past his prime. "He'd sit in camp and drink No. 4 Scotch all day and send his four crack Swiss guides to climb a mountain," said Simpson. "When they came back to camp and reported he'd then sit down and write a damn fine article for the CPR."

Empty the mountains were not. That was the convenient fantasy. Wide open, maybe. How else would there have been the kind of collecting that saw Burgess Shale fossils shipped off to the Smithsonian Institution in Washington, DC, just as fast as the pack horses could get them down the trail? Curiously, in the first decades of the 20th century, the "disappearing red man" was added to the romance, perhaps in tacit acknowledgment that the "nonexistent Indian" narrative had become untenable. Now, according to government pamphlets, Native peoples had bequeathed charming legends, and their half-buried dwellings sat at the base of Mount Rundle "where now the tourist plays golf."

The hot springs at Banff, "discovered" by white settlers and eventually becoming the property of the federal government, had been in use for millennia. Trails and passes, same thing. Archaeological digs begun in the 1970s at the Vermilion Lakes reveal nearly 11,000 years of human use. True, archaeologists had not begun to dig in Mabel Williams's day, but she was wrong even according to what was known in her time.

But the mountain parks – vast, inspiring and uncharted – had a purpose in their earliest days, and that purpose was to heal and soothe white people. When Jasper National Park was created, the Métis were evicted. The case of Ewan Moberly and his family is now cited as an example of the great unfairness of government. He and his people (defined as "half-breeds" and "squatters," although there was at the time no possibility of their registering title on their lands) were trespassing on a dream. That which did not serve the dream was removed. Bounties were put on wolves and coyotes, because those species were thought to reduce the numbers of the animals hunters preferred. The government did not question that it was correct.

This idea of emptiness, of sacredness, was only the first fantasy of the Rockies. Natural beauty would salve the soul, that was where we began. Then society became a little more cynical and, anyway, money was needed. That spiritual balm could attract tourist dollars. The beauty spots could be commercialized. Tourism will save us. That fantasy had a run of many decades until it, too, lost its lustre. Next we adopted the eco-fantasy and its child, the wildlife fantasy. Old fantasies don't exactly die, but they become backup. They are most of them good ideas. Too bad that when a new one comes it threatens to cancel out the others.

I've been reading about the first white people in these mountains, in letters and diaries at the far-sighted, privately founded Whyte Museum of the Canadian Rockies. On audiotapes created by the Luxton Foundation, I've heard the high falsetto "Oh sure!" of Jimmy Simpson, and the thoughtful tones of Louis Trono, a musician who was born in Bankhead, the coal mining town that once stood above Lake Minnewanka. Men worked in coal mines all day, then showered off the soot and donned white ties to play in a swing band at the Banff Springs Hotel. What lives! And so recent, less than 150 years ago, 100 years ago, men and women who are alive in the memories of many.

I admit, some of these "first" people, pioneers and adventurers, can be a bit tiresome. They are the entitled: they had all the glory to themselves. They arrived when the park was pristine; they were suckers for the sublime.

Their narratives repeat myths of the "vanishing red man," the hunted-out game, the poison of encroaching civilization. But they did learn and understand and glory in this place. I wonder if the current attitude to them is tinged with envy. Why should they have had freedoms we don't? They learned trails from the Natives, and passed them down to us. But who wanted trails anyway, people say today. It is hard to disagree that roads and railways – the national dream – have led to the decline of Banff, Jasper, Yoho and Kootenay parks. The mountains have been democratized. They are for the people, and there are too many of us.

The road to democracy in the Rocky Mountain parks has been a twisting one. Promoting the health of Canadians weary of their cities and in need of fresh air and beautiful scenery seemed simple. But there was a question of industry: Include it because the railways need coal? Exclude it because it's ugly? What about forests? In 1911 the Dominion Forest Reserves and Parks Act defined parks as surrounded by forest reserves. Parks would encourage development; reserves would "look to the exclusion of people." The inner Rocky Mountains Park was shrunk to about 40 per cent of its former area.

Gateposts moved. And what was allowed through the gates changed. Cars had been prohibited; in 1910, they were allowed in. Bankhead was part of the fantasy, with electric lights and running water and a school and churches and a hotel: the houses were better built than those in Banff. Tourists might come and have a look. But Bankhead operated for little more than ten years. In 1922, there was a strike. The CPR closed the mine and the whole town was demolished, the better buildings hauled on flatbed trucks to Banff. The town was erased.

If you have an enchanted kingdom, surely one of the key powers is deciding what's in and what's out. As a chapter by Alan MacEachern in *A Century of Parks Canada* notes, Mabel Williams, by her own admission, came up with the next great idea. She found some minutes of the Scenic and Historic Preservation Society of America: one of the "old chaps" got up and said, "You know, when you think of it, these beautiful places are worth money. [They] bring people in to see them." She carried the idea to her boss. "Tourist traffic" became the rationale for parks in the face of government indifference. Harkin even came up with a figure: scenery was worth $13.88 an acre (wheatfields came in at $4.91).

So parks were for tourists. Cars were in. Roads were in. (Horse travel nearly out.) During the 1920s, promotional literature brought in the glamorous visitors, the golf courses, the movie stars. But there were other activities permitted in those large tracts of empty land, out of sight of most Canadians, not so attractive. Prison camps, for instance. Already, in the First World War, Ukrainian Canadians had been interned at Castle Mountain. In the 1930s a large government tent city of the unemployed assembled around Morley. In the 1940s the parks were pretty well left alone – except as prisoner of war camps. In the Second World War, German prisoners cleared what is now Barrier Lake in the Kananaskis. You can see the guard tower of Camp 130 in the Kananaskis and walk through the bush to see the lines of the barbed wire fences that marked the playing field. But of the tent city, of the First World War camp at Cave and Basin in Banff townsite, there is nothing. It is as if they never existed.

After the war, in the sunny 1950s, Canadian families pulled up to the gates in their cars. Kids could watch the bears eat at the town dump in Jasper, as I did. We rode up to Sunshine in a Brewster bus with skis rattling in the outside rack. On certain hairpin turns, you had to get out and stand off the road while the men pushed. It was such fun.

Everyone caught on. By the 1960s the campgrounds were overflowing. Tunnel Mountain campground in Banff was party city. Ski resorts burgeoned, and sewage seeped into the creeks below Sunshine Village. Ecological notions were in the air, although park wardens still had the authority to shoot predators on sight. Scientists were invoked, strangely for the first time.

At the 1968 conference "Canadian National Parks: Today and Tomorrow," the highly respected zoologist Ian McTaggart-Cowan – who had roamed for several summers with Jimmy Simpson – laid it out bluntly. "Ecological considerations had almost no part in the establishment of the Canadian National Parks." He cited past mistakes in managing parks, such as selling off the land in the river valleys, areas the large mammals needed. He talked about fighting wildfires, because by then we knew wildfires were beneficial for forest areas. We might have learned this from Native peoples, but we did not pay attention at the time – it was not fashionable to do so. He pointed out the conflicting motives in parks management, and his timing was right.

The idea of parks protecting nature took hold. Public consultations were arranged. By 2000 a new National Parks Act held as its first priority the "maintenance or restoration of ecological integrity." It was a new fashion and it appears to be on a collision course with the previous ones.

The billboard catches your eye when you leave Calgary driving west: "You are in Grizzly Country." In this scheme of things, people are an impediment to nature. Either we're "windshield visitors," or we're clogging up the campgrounds and leaving our footprints and endangering wildlife.

Parks now have a dual mandate of conservation and recreation. If these ideas aren't mutually defeating, they are at least hard to reconcile. In the 21st century, voices of environmentalism and of science have become louder. They have contributed much to the conversation. New protections are in place. But now there is a profession of parks people and a new language. You can't draw a line around a piece of nature and save it: this is, in the parlance of the professionals, "othering" nature. "Islandizing" nature. Parks are "the incarceration of wilderness." What about the Rocky Mountain parks belonging, as in the original vision, to the people of Canada? What about the transformative power of this wild place, for people? In the current version, if we are not nature's jailers, then we are its defilers.

And so we are asked to leave Eden. Trails close or fall into neglect and hikers are unhappy. Or the opposite happens – some overnight accommodation is allowed at Maligne Lake, which Mary Schäffer found by following

Samson Beaver's map. The parks-should-be-pristine camp is equally furious. Even the animals have given their wordless disapproval: says *Grizzly Manifesto* author Jeff Gailus, the bears are safer living outside park boundaries altogether, for instance in northern Alberta.

A couple of questions: How close were Canadians to being transformed by living in the mountains, or even spending time here? Not very close. In fact, today more than 90 per cent of park visitors go no farther than 250 metres from a road. And that's a good thing: if everyone hiked the trails, the backcountry would collapse under the strain. Mind you, no one really knows what the acceptable "load" is on the backcountry. It hasn't been studied; there's no money to study it. There are quotas on the numbers of people who can take the amazing hike over Jasper's Skyline Trail. If that doesn't discourage you, filthy washrooms and tortuous access – via the nine-kilometre disused fire road you have to take to get on or off the trail – put off all but the most devoted. Can parks have it both ways, reaching out to new visitors while discouraging their oldest friends?

And, anyway, goes this line of thinking, those guys from the past were politically incorrect, weren't they? They hunted grizzlies and bighorn sheep and picked wildflowers. They built their little cabins up in the passes and their nasty little shacks by the riverbanks. Their horses gouged out the ground around the trails. The parks that gave them free rein were elitist. You had to have money; activities like skiing and golf were allowed, while others, like snowmobiling, were not.

And so the argument goes. Parks proponents were

to get rid of the traces of human history. A case in point was Wheeler House, which existed, until three years ago, in Banff. It was the summer home of Arthur Wheeler, grandfather of the local climbing community. It had been standing vacant for years. Parks Canada decided to demolish it. Jenny Compton, Arthur's great-grand-daughter, told the parks commissioner she would raise the money to save it. But the house stood in a newly designated wildlife corridor. So, despite protests and promises, it was doomed.

Another superintendent, at another moment in time, might have chosen to restore this historic home so that park visitors could visit and learn some human history. But, no. He was in the grip of an idea. Wildlife needed its newly defined corridor. People should not clutter the landscape with their dwellings. The people of today aren't to see the human marks upon this place.

Before it was knocked down, the family created a foundation and sent in artists to memorialize the house: watercolours and photographs show a charming log cabin with a pond set among trees. And they are all that remain.

This park is a fresh slate. Nobody lived here. What will it be now?

Yes, it is definitely time to change the fantasy. Aesthetics are out of fashion. Elites are out of fashion. Pioneers stepped out of line. Spiritual bliss isn't really offered anymore: no one visits babbling brooks in alpine meadows except in a shampoo ad. Now we have new utilitarian rationales for national parks. And yet they have a familiar ring. In Australia, the parks system is directly seen as linked to the health system. "Feeling blue? Touch green." People are literally prescribed visits to nature if they're depressed or ill. Are we heading this way?

Parks have been "ableist," the theorists now say. That is, they aren't accessible to those with disabilities. So we have wheelchair walks, and we have the much-reviled, much-debated Glacier Skywalk at the Columbia Icefields. We have via ferrata. And we have urban outreach.

So what do we now believe about parks? The reigning fantasy is one I would call Parks Without Borders/ Parcs Sans Frontières. The idea is expansionist. Wildlife migration routes encourage thinkers toward linking parks and reaching out to more territory. There is Y2Y, with its aim to connect the parks from Yellowstone to Yukon. We will bring back bison. There are plans to restore Aboriginal presence. Remote places, natural and wilder places, seem to offer lessons on how we might manage the rest of our earthly territory. Everywhere, we see clues about what is to come.

Our wonderful friends the artists have been an enduring presence in the parks since the CPR commissioned Marmaduke Matthews to paint scenery as the tracks pushed west and the Group of Seven wandered around Yoho's Lake O'Hara. And the artists are still with us. But they're not after beauty anymore. Jan Kabatoff paints retreating glaciers out of a concern for climate change. I asked Nancy Townshend, author of the forthcoming *Artistic Responses to the Canadian Rockies, Purcell Mountains and Selkirk Mountains 1809–2012*, what she thought was the new vision. "Maybe parks will save the world," she said.

But playing God is tricky. You can get tripped up in your ideologies. *Park* as a word is easy to fill and empty, to inflate, to inflect, to present in sacred light; on the ground, it's messier. One keel remains in the wobbling ship that is Parks Canada, and that is the tenet of emptiness. Today, no one in Parks management has much use for Banff townsite. It has "zero conservation value," one Parks insider tells me. Perhaps. But it has huge historical value, and continues to despite the number of teardowns – the Frank Lloyd Wright–designed pavilion, demolished in 1938, is one that comes to mind.

We have seen the dangers of whole landscapes, living environments, guided by the hand of man when the hand of man is guided by politics and fashion, when testimony and the traces of the people who knew the place best are forgotten. We have done that before. I'm just asking: What if, like Mabel Williams, our very contemporary, seemingly convincing, ideas are wrong? Can we move from fantasy to reality?

BANFF KIDS

Miki Kawano

Banff is one of the two main towns in the Bow Valley, and the kids that live there are interesting. I guess you might call us ignorant, or maybe even a little weird. The kids who are born and raised in this little town have quite a different perspective than the average child. We're strange individuals; it's like we've been living under a rock our whole lives, isolated and unknowing of what's actually out in the real world.

I was one of those ignorant Banff kids. Born and raised in the Bow Valley, I always thought that my life was pretty normal, and that most children grew up the same way I did.

Growing up in Banff, I was always surrounded by mountains. I've never lived in a place without them. Wasn't it normal to live in a mountain range? In Grade 5 science, I remember learning about the "grasslands" and "prairies," but as a kid I didn't think that people *actually* lived there. During the winter months, skiing wasn't exactly a choice for me. Whether I wanted to go or not, I woke up at seven and was put in the car half-asleep with my snow pants in one hand and my helmet in the other. I didn't even like skiing that much when I was younger. I mostly went just so I could get cookies and hot chocolate at the end of the day. Since my parents were both ski instructors, I always got a free season's pass to Norquay, Sunshine and Lake Louise – the three main ski areas in the Bow Valley – and, until I was about 12, I didn't even know ski passes were something you paid for! Summertime in the valley was no different. It was a dreadful season because in my family summer meant hiking. *Ugh, so much effort.* For Banff kids, hiking was just one of those things that you did, not because you wanted to but because you *had* to. It was a real mystery to my sister and I why people went hiking for fun.

A small community in a national park has its pros and cons, but it can give people unusual little opportunities that you may or may not be able to experience anywhere else. Something like having the mayor's cell-phone number, debating before town council whether parking should be free or having a bear take a nap in your backyard – believe it or not – is all pretty normal in the life of a "Banffite." Going for a run and having to make a detour around a herd of bull elk is considered normal. This might sound crazy, but one time when it was particularly cold outside, we found a deer trying to sneak into the school to warm up. If it was minus 40 degrees Celsius and if I was a deer, I'd probably be doing the same thing. Another thing most kids don't get to experience very often is making the cover of the local newspaper. Pretty much every single Banff kid has been in the *Crag & Canyon* or the *Rocky Mountain Outlook* at least once in their childhood. Whether it's for artwork, sports or community events, it's been a common occurrence in the 18 years I've lived here in Banff.

As I got older, I slowly came out from beneath the rock I'd been living under all my life and realized that my life was actually far from ordinary.

It all started when I attended school in Japan for the first time—to gain "experience," according to my grandmother. I was extremely shocked to see how different the schools in Japan were compared to back in Banff. Since our community is so small, the size of our school is minuscule compared to the average school. Of course, I was unaware of that at the time. In my 8-year-old mind, all schools were the same as my school: 300 kids, each grade with around 50 kids, give or take, and everybody knew each other. I remember when I first arrived in Japan being overwhelmed by the sheer number of students—five classes of 35 kids in just a single grade!

Since I had never gone to school anywhere else, I believed that Banff school rules were still in effect. Here in Banff, it is not uncommon for kids to miss school on a "powder day." In Japan? You'd probably get expelled if you missed school to go skiing. All of this made me start to realize how different Banff kids are.

Calgary is only 128 kilometres from Banff, yet the lifestyle there is very different. For an inexperienced Banff kid like me, "the city life" is something we don't quite understand. Take public transit, for example. Public transit is actually an extremely terrifying thing for us, because we have absolutely no idea how to use it. We've never had to use it growing up here, and, until recently, Banff didn't even have any form of it. Transfers, train tickets and bus stops are all very confusing for me. We can find our way through the backcountry wilderness but not through Calgary's transit system. Imagine me sitting on a bus, nervous because I don't know where to get off and confused about whether I should press the stop button or not. That's the image you'd be seeing if the average Banff kid tried to navigate around Calgary using public transit.

Something that I always took for granted as a child was how blessed we are to live in such a safe environment. I basically thought that everywhere was as safe as Banff, because I'd never experienced anything dangerous growing up here. The most violent thing I'd ever witnessed in elementary school was when two boys decided it would be fun to throw scissors at each other. I learned over time, however, that gang fights and teens bringing weapons to school are not particularly uncommon in Calgary. Some time ago, a few of my Calgary friends were talking about a knife fight that had happened in their school, where apparently one of the three boys had been stabbed. What surprised me was not the fact that it actually happened but the fact that they were talking about it like it was nothing out of the ordinary. For someone who grew up in such a safe, tight-knit community as Banff, it was unbelievable.

Recently, I was fortunate enough to go on a five-week program in Jonquière, Quebec, to improve my French and learn about the culture. There, I stayed with a host family, which was really beneficial to improving my speaking. However, their house was much further from the school than I had anticipated. As a Banff kid, I've never lived more than a three-minute walk from my school, and I couldn't believe that I had to bike half an hour every single day just to get there! It's weird growing up in such a small town, because you get used to everything being so close together. School, my friend's house, the grocery store and even the campgrounds are all within walking distance from each other. Biking everywhere for five weeks was a rather exhausting experience.

Drinking water is another common concern for a Banff kid. We are probably the fussiest group of people you'll ever meet when it comes to tap water. The "Banff water" that we locals can't live without comes straight from clean, clear springs in the mountains. Every Banff kid understands the pain of bringing three full bottles when going to Nowhere, Alberta, because we don't approve of their inferior tap water. Growing up with such clean, high-quality water, and with such a sensitive system, no wonder I got sick from drinking the water in Quebec.

During my stay in Quebec, I met many people my age from across the country. What was really cool about this was that everybody – and I mean EVERYBODY – knew about Banff National Park. I was famous just because of where I was from. My host family, friends and teachers were all extremely jealous that I lived in Banff. The thing is, I'd never even thought of being lucky to live here. It's just Banff, just a place I've lived my whole life. That's the weird thing about us Banff kids, we get so used to our surroundings that we don't ever think to appreciate it.

Driving back from the airport into the valley, I was truly fascinated by the beauty and size of our mountains. It was like I was seeing them for the first time. The very first thing I did when I got back home was snap a picture of Cascade Mountain – I felt like a tourist in my own town. Five weeks away from home made me realize just how fortunate I am to live in this beautiful valley.

Banff kids are interesting kids. They don't know how to take public transit, they complain about tap water and they don't know any big-city rules. I guess you could call them sheltered, and maybe even a little weird, but that's what makes these kids special. The small community, the great mountains and the valuable things they can only experience in Banff give them a path to become unique individuals.

I was one of those ignorant Banff kids, and now that I have tasted the world outside this valley, I realize how lucky I am to be one.

THE NAKODA AND MY CHANGING PERSPECTIVES

John Reilly

I have lived in the valley of the Bow for almost 25 years, since the Alberta government transferred me here from Calgary to be the resident Provincial Court judge. Getting that transfer was like winning a lottery. Unfortunately, this valley is such a desirable place to live that the price of real estate has risen to a point where, for many people, winning a lottery would be the only way they could afford to come here.

My favourite place in the valley is Grassi Lakes, two little tarns up in White Man's Pass. The round trip from the parking lot to the lakes is about a three-kilometre walk and a height gain of a little under 1,000 feet. I find it to be a perfect bit of exercise and I have done it over a thousand times. If you climb above the upper lake, there are pictographs believed to have been made by young Stoneys on vision quests. I love to imagine those days when the Stoneys followed their traditional spiritualism in this valley before the intrusion of the white man.

My work as the resident judge in Canmore made me the circuit judge for the towns of Banff and Cochrane, and gave me jurisdiction over all of the cases that arose on the Stoney Indian Reserve at Morley. Lying just east of the mountains, in the foothills, and occupying a large swath of grasslands, it was still called the "Stoney Indian Reserve" when I arrived. That was the 1990s, and it was a time of change in the awareness of Indigenous peoples, both in themselves and as they were perceived by the non-Indigenous population.

As part of that changing awareness, many Native communities now call themselves by names that are in their original language. The Stoney are Nakoda Sioux. There are three dialects of Sioux: the Nakoda, the Lakota and the Dakota. I have heard some say that they came to this area after the Battle of the Little Bighorn, but that was 1876, and the Stoney were here in the mid-1700s, when Anthony Henday visited this area. They likely came here in the 1500s to escape the diseases that were brought by Europeans and that so ravaged their communities. They now refer to the reserve as the Stoney Nakoda First Nations.

I detest the final s in that name. It is my perspective that the division of the people at Morley into three separate "First Nations" is the work of greedy men who seek to keep the divisions, so they can exploit and control parts of it, because they know that they cannot control all of it.

In 1972 there was an attempt to unite the reserve

under one chief. The main aspirants for the position of chief during that year's election were the Rev. Dr. John Snow and Frank Kaquitts. Kaquitts won to become the chief of the whole reserve. John Snow, upon realizing that he would not be chief, lied to his people. He told them that because three chiefs signed the treaty, the Stoney Nakoda would lose their treaty rights if they did not maintain three chiefs. There was no truth to this. There were, in fact, five Stoney signatories to Treaty 7 when it was signed at Blackfoot Crossing – south and east of what is today Calgary – in 1877. The treaty rights, such as they are, are inalienable whether the Stoney have one chief or 30. But the lie stuck. I have spoken to a number of the Elders who insist it is true. I don't believe these Elders are lying; they simply believed the lie and now repeat it in all honesty. But the damage was done.

There was a time when I felt a little envious of the people who lived in those quaint-looking houses on the whalebacks along the highway. Their sites, often shared by herds of horses, looked very pastoral from a distance. But as a judge I got a much closer look. I became aware of a less peaceful aspect of reserve life through the many cases that came before my court. In trying to understand the disproportionate number of violent crimes committed on the reserve, I tried to get to know the people who lived in those houses. I learned that many of the occupants lived in poverty and social dysfunction. I learned of the history of colonialism that has so damaged the social fabric of the Indigenous people.

To see the roots of the damage done by colonialism, and how it has impacted the Nakoda people, we have to look back to Canada's original colonist. I saw the harm that was done to these people through the genocidal policies of the Aryan racist John A. Macdonald, our first prime minister.

Now when I look at those houses, I feel anger to think that so many of the occupants of those homes are so disadvantaged. I believe the descendants of the original occupiers of this land should enjoy a special place in our society, but instead most are amongst the poorest in our country.

There was a time when I thought my father's comment about Macdonald as the "brandy-swilling Orangeman who murdered Louis Riel" was an exaggeration motivated by his loyalty to the Liberal Party and his family connection to Louis St. Laurent, the Liberal prime minister from 1948 to 1957. When I read the Royal Commission on Aboriginal Peoples and learned that Macdonald announced in the Canadian Parliament that he would assimilate the Indian people so that it would be "as if the tribal society had never existed," I understood the truth in my father's perception. In a recent article in the *National Post*, Canadian historian Tim Stanley is quoted as saying that "Macdonald's were among the most extreme views of his era. He was the only politician in the parliamentary debates to refer to Canada as 'Aryan' and to justify legalized racism on the basis not of alleged cultural practices but on the grounds that 'Chinese' and 'Aryans' were separate species."

The low point in Macdonald's career must have been on November 5, 1873, when he was forced to resign as prime minister because he and his party had taken over

$35,000 in bribes (about $7 million in today's terms) from an investor who wanted to secure the contract to build the CPR. He initially denied this until it was proven that he personally had asked for and received payment. His party evidently didn't see anything wrong with what he had done. They refused to accept his offer to resign as leader. He became prime minister again ... and went on to complete the railway ... and murder Louis Riel.

Now I think my father's comment understated the evil of the man.

There was a time when I thought the sound of a freight train steaming through the valley was exciting and romantic.

Now I think of how horrifying it must have been for Stoney Nakoda people who were my age in 1885, the year the railroad was completed. They had lived their lives on a prairie that was quiet and peaceful and where huge herds of buffalo provided them with all the necessities of their lives. The rumble of the steam engines, the belching smoke, the fires caused by sparks from those engines and all the white settlers that came on those trains were the end of their way of life. Now I think of this when I hear a train, and the sound fills me with sadness.

There was also a time when I saw our justice system as an ideal, a system that treated rich and poor, strong and weak equally – levelled the playing field for all. Then I learned about the treatment of the Indigenous people. Colonization – the application of a foreign system of law on a people without their consent. In trying to understand why the people at Morley were so over-represented in my courts, I learned that many of them saw my glorious justice system as an instrument of their oppression. I saw the inherent lack of fairness and lack of equality in a system that applied laws to a people who had no say in the creation of those laws or the courts that applied them.

There was a time when I thought the punishment of crime was a good thing. I believed that punishments would have the effect of deterring a wrongdoer and others from the wrongdoing. Twenty years of watching the same offenders at Morley appear before me again and again showed me the futility of what I was doing. I think the most disheartening thing for me was seeing a man I had sentenced to prison a number of times in the '80s come into court with his son, the son now charged with the same kind of offence. The cycle of despair and hopelessness literally being handed down from father to son.

I was impressed by the words of Chief Seattle: "We did not weave the web of life, we are but strands within it, whatever we do to the web we do to ourselves." When we just convict offenders of crimes and throw them in prison, without dealing with the underlying cause and the long history that has resulted in the commission of their crimes, we fail to protect the web. The offenders are part of the web of human life.

The basic difference between the Indigenous concept of justice and the European one is that the European system sees wrongdoing as a deliberate act that deserves punishment; Indigenous people see wrongdoing as ignorance in need of teaching or an illness in need of healing. What I saw every day in my courtrooms confirmed this as absolutely true. The offenders needed help, teaching and healing. It was the abuses they suffered that were the cause of their wrongdoing. Adding more abuse to their lives was not the solution, it merely contributed to the continuation of the problem.

What I came to see was that the majority of the people who came before me charged with criminal offences were not bad people, they were just ordinary people who made mistakes and needed help to deal with the circumstances of their lives. It made me so disagree with our punishment-oriented criminal justice system that in spite of the ridiculously generous remuneration I received, I could no longer be a part of it.

So now I have more time to enjoy the forests that the Stoney once called home, and here, too, my perspective has changed. I like to build things that don't require meticulous finishing, like fences and decks. There was a time when I would hike in the forests and I would look at the trees and think about how many two-by-fours and two-by-sixes could be cut out of them. The Indigenous people have taught me the concept of wholeness and the interrelatedness of creation. Now I look at those trees and I think about the carbon dioxide that I breathe out and they breathe in, and the oxygen that they breathe out and I breathe in. The people and the place are inextricably linked as part of the web of life. I am just beginning to understand the sacred beauty of my surroundings.

THE GREAT UNCERTAINTY

Stephen Legault

The flood of 2013 has receded. I live near the headwaters of the Bow River, in Canmore, near the border of Banff National Park, and less than 700 metres as the crow flies from the now-infamous Cougar Creek. Most days, the Bow River along this reach is a swift-moving, deep blue vein that pulses between banks of spruce and pine, along aspen meadows and past clutches of willow.

Since Wednesday (June 19), it's been a wide, brown and spreading conveyor belt of trees, rock, silt and mud that has enveloped everything in its path. Its feeder creeks, like Cougar Creek, are normally ephemeral, rising for a few weeks in the spring to deposit snowmelt and spring rain, and a few truckloads of gravel, into the main stem of the river.

Not this spring.

Life is uncertain. This is one of the fundamental tenets of human existence. We don't know what's going to happen. We know that someday we're going to die, but we don't know when. We know, in our gut, that everything that is important to us – our children, our partners, our parents, our friends and family, and, yes, even those material objects that we clutch at with such desperation – will one day vanish, before or at the moment of our own demise.

We know that life is change, but our difficulty accepting that truth causes no end of suffering in our day-to-day lives.

On Thursday morning, many of us in Canmore woke up to learn how real that axiom really is, as Cougar Creek, dry for 50 weeks of the year and usually contained between its engineered banks of trap-rock and fill, had carved a new course through the residential community that bears its name. The creek, a few metres wide during a normal spring runoff, surged to more than 75 metres, tearing a wide rent through its historic alluvial fan and making off with people's backyards, sheds, fences and eventually foundations. That no homes toppled into the creek is a miracle.

Cougar Creek and dozens of others – Exshaw, Heart, Jura, Three Sisters, Pigeon – all amassed their flows into the Bow, and meeting with the Kananaskis, Ghost and Elbow rivers, the Bow flooded a vast area of downtown Calgary.

And on it went: Turner Valley, Black Diamond, Bragg Creek, Kananaskis, Morley; maybe the hardest hit was High River, where the entire town was evacuated and underwater. Lives were lost, the financial cost of the damage estimated at $6 billion, the most expensive natural disaster in Canadian history.

During the height of the flood, we were evacuated from our east Cougar Creek neighbourhood. The flood has given us this new name for where we live. As crews worked valiantly to save the bridge over Cougar Creek, the 900 or so residents who live on the eastern bank of the creek's alluvial fan were loaded on buses and shipped out over the fragile structure. We watched as all that water, the colour of chocolate pudding, pounded against the road, the embankment and the seemingly too-narrow culvert that went under them.

Years ago I hiked up Exshaw Creek, into the South Ghost River, and down Cougar Creek from its head-waters with author and geologist Ben Gadd. Ben lived in Jasper then, and upon seeing the multimillion-dollar homes built on the outside bank of Cougar Creek, and the inadequacy of the culvert under the road, said something to the effect that they wouldn't last.

Work crews laboured around the clock to save that bridge. They did. How remains a mystery, and one of the greatest success stories of that first day of the deluge, but on Thursday it looked very much in doubt.

As the water rose that afternoon, we shut off the gas, power and water to our house, packed a few bags with everything from our marriage certificate to sleeping bags and left.

Life is uncertain. We had no idea what would happen if the rumours were true that officials were considering a scenario where they might divert Cougar Creek down Elk Run Boulevard to prevent it from breaching the bridge. Elk Run is long, straight and steep, and the velocity of water rushing down it would have been uncontrollable. Our home would have been just a hundred feet from that spillway.

Nor did we know when we'd be able to return home, if we had a home to return to, or what condition it might be in if it was still standing. We put everything of value on the third floor, closed the door and walked away.

We spent three days and two nights at a friend – Gareth Thomson's – home, ironically just a hundred feet from the floodwaters behind the dyke along the banks of the Bow River. We stocked up on groceries, put aside a lot of water, bought beer, wine and tequila (the latter is a critical item on the list of supplies to have on hand in case of any emergency) and settled in.

Through all of this, my mother – who arrived on Wednesday night, and noted as we drove into town that the creek looked awfully wide, and wondered what all the fire trucks and police cars were doing on the Cougar Creek bridge – remained stoic. Sure, she had a few minutes here and there, as we all did, spent in frustration, but in general she went with the flow. So to speak.

Gareth, Jenn and I spent Friday driving around town, offering to help people in need, carrying their stuff (and holy crap do people have a lot of crap, but that's another story) out of basements and garages at risk of flooding.

Friday afternoon I took a panicked call from someone just a few streets away, saying that the Minnewanka Dam had breached and that we had to evacuate immediately. We threw our gear into the back of Gareth's car: whatever we had packed, along with some valuables, computers, my camera, my mom. Someone grabbed a box of granola bars and I grabbed the beer. We abandoned the tequila to the expected deluge.

Five minutes later we got another call. No dam had breached; it was only some rising water along the street. We noted that the children still frolicked in the lake-sized puddles, a surreal scene. We unpacked nothing but the beer, which we proceeded to drink in Gareth's driveway.

Saturday we were allowed to return home. Not a drop of water got into our house, and the bridge over Cougar Creek remained standing, though the landscape around it will be forever changed, as will the lives of all those who lived along its banks.

Life is uncertain; we don't know what will happen, or when we will die, and what will happen when we do. But there are foundations on which we build our existence, and for millennia humankind has based how we live on certain assumptions. One assumption is that nature has patterns that can be predicted and that we can shape our lives around.

That is no longer the case.

Climate change changes the game; all the assumptions we have made about where we live and how we carry out our lives must be thrown into the flood and a new set of assumptions created. The problem for humanity is that we like predictability, even if it is myth. Climate change reveals the hoax of this way of life.

Hurricane Katrina, the floods in Pakistan, Superstorm Sandy, two-kilometre-wide tornados; these and a thousand other instances of bizarre, destructive, random and seemingly unpredictable weather events are the new norm, and from the perspective of people trying to live as we always have – where we crave certainty – they are anathema to our sense of security.

In the wake of the floods of 2013, Canmore, Calgary and every other community affected have come together to work as a family to clean up and rebuild. I've got my tools in the back of my car, and when I see someone posting that they need help, I drop what I'm doing and head out the door. In Calgary, a posting for 300 volunteers nets 5,000. That's how we're going to get through the next year or two: working together. We use our hearts and our heads and our skills.

We're going to need a whole new set of skills, and to reinvent some old ones, to cope with what is coming. We'll need to learn how to build bridges, fortify river banks, build on higher ground, store food, use less, love more and remember that we're all living downstream, in nature, surrounded by both the causes and consequences of our actions.

Maybe the most important skill we'll need to face the Great Uncertainty that climate change presents is to sit with the knowledge that we simply won't know what's going to happen next.

PART FOUR

The Wild Side

GREEN EYES ON THE
GOAT CREEK TRAIL

Kristy Davison

Each winter, in deepest, darkest January, my friend
Amy and I plan a full-moon cross-country ski trip from
Canmore to Banff via the Goat Creek Trail. The trail,
roughly 20 kilometres of easy skiing, runs behind the
Rundle range and connects the two towns. It's a popular
trail on sunny Rocky Mountain winter days, but we had
never encountered another soul on it in the years we've
been skiing it by night.

The first year we attempted this adventure we timed
it perfectly with the moonrise. The full moon rose above
Mount Rundle just as the last of the sun's light was
fading. It glowed so brightly that we were able to ski
the entire distance without headlamps. The air felt like
breathing pure moonlight. We felt humbly privileged to
be on a journey amongst such simple, natural wonders.
We vowed to make this trip an annual occurrence.

Later attempts, however, never worked out quite as well as they did on that first ski. One year, Amy managed to scratch her eyeball on the handle of her ski pole in a particularly spectacular crash. She skied the rest of that trip with one eye open. For a few years, the cloud cover prevented a full moonlight experience. Our expectations may have been a little too lofty considering the triumphs of that first year's five-star tour.

And then there was the year that the moon didn't rise at all. That was the year when this particular story took place; a dark time in our history on the Goat Creek Trail.

∧ ∧ ∧

Our tradition is to leave work a little early so we can set out from the trailhead around 4:30 p.m., just as the short-lived light of the winter's day is dwindling. The biggest threat on the route is one steep, sharp corner leading down to the first bridge near the beginning of the trail, and it is always preferable for hacks like us to sacrifice ourselves to that icy slope while we still have a bit of light to work with.

We set out on this clear, brisk, late afternoon, smiles on our faces, our packs brimming with extra layers, dark chocolate bars, thermoses of Bengal Spice tea, beef jerky and a few coins for celebratory brews from the Banff Springs liquor store at journey's end.

The snow was pristine: a good grip on the uphills but smooth enough to provide plenty of giddy speed on the downhill sections. We were making good time, chatting about life and hooting and hollering our way down the switchbacks that lead to the approximate halfway point at the Spray River bridge.

By the time we reached the Spray, the sun was long gone. Our eyes were continually adjusting to the deepening darkness, so we decided to keep skiing a bit further without pulling out our headlamps, hoping against hope that the moon would rise above the wall of mountains, once again lighting our way.

But it never did.

Before we knew it, any light that had been lingering in the spruce trees had completely vanished. We could barely see the ends of our skis and were moving forward into the darkness by instinct and the feel of our feet in the subtle tracks grooved by other skiers.

Reluctantly accepting that we would not be graced by moonlight once again, we pulled up beside each other and flopped our packs on the snow. We'd have a quick tea and a snack and then strap on our headlamps for the remainder of the route to Banff.

We were enjoying some beef jerky when we heard a heavy crunching sound in the snow to the right of the track from where we stood. The sound came from just 20 metres away. Moments later, there was another footstep. And another. Moving. Slowly.

We froze.

"Oh, shit. Did you hear that?" I whispered without moving a muscle.

"Yeah. That was *big*," Amy confirmed.

We were blind, ten kilometres from Banff and roughly the same distance from Canmore. The smart thing would have been to take a second to pull out our lamps, but it seems the instinctive flight response trumped good judgment. We threw our packs on and skied frantically into the darkness in the opposite direction of the sinister sounds.

That plan lasted about two minutes because we had to stop and deal with our light situation: we couldn't even tell if we were skiing the right direction, toward Banff, on the track. So we dropped our bags and groped for our headlamps, snapping them on. A signpost along the track reflected in the small beam of light, giving us our bearings. At least we were headed in the right direction!

The ice cracked and moaned at the river's edge, echoing footfalls of something heavy and wild. Whatever was out there was following us.

"Let's go!" we yelped simultaneously.

We didn't say a word as we skied into the dark. The narrative running through my mind for the next hour, however, as I constantly scanned the forest for eyes, involved a complex feat of engineering in which I would construct a rescue sled from our skis and backpack straps, so that I could strap Amy's mangled body to it and drag her to Banff after the beast had had its way with her. In my mind, the design of this sled was pure genius: smooth and strong, something an Inuit hunter would be proud of. Roomy enough for two large seals. Needless to say, an hour is a long time to be trapped inside your imagination in the deep, dark woods.

Thankfully, as we skied with what was left of our energy toward what we hoped was safety, we began to recognize some of the turns as the final kilometre or so of the trail. Maybe we weren't going to be lost to the forest after all.

As we came closer and closer to the end of the trail, the tension and focus slowly began to melt away. We broke the silence: I admitted, "Oh, man. I have been freaking out. Were you scared? I was scared."

"I wasn't *that* scared," Amy lied.

I told her about the part of my plan that involved popping our skis off as quickly as possible so that we could use them as pitiful, awkward weapons should a death struggle ensue. We started to laugh, and she told me how the fact that I kept pointing my light into the woods was really freaking her out, but she was too out of breath to say anything.

We were mid-laugh when we saw the eyes.

Caught in the light of our lamps, right in the middle of the trail, not 40 metres ahead of us, gleamed a pair of bright green eyes. Unblinking eyes two feet off the ground; they were slowly, but brazenly, creeping toward us.

We stopped in our tracks, completely paralyzed. Instead of popping our skis off for a fight to the death as per my brilliant plan, we instead began screaming like we had never screamed before. These screams – the sounds falling somewhere on the spectrum between mother grizzly and the screech of a golden eagle – welled up from the very depths of our animal souls.

Still, the eyes moved closer, fearless, wild, unaffected by our shrieking.

This is it, I said to myself. This is the way I'm going

to die. The worst possible scenario that I have been imagining for the last hour is actually about to unfold. Screaming suddenly felt futile.

As the wild thing continued to approach, our attempts at scaring the creature clearly futile, we stopped our yelling, frozen and unsure of what to do next. Then, a small, confused voice cut through the dark: "Uh ... hello?"

The thing was close enough now to emerge into the cone of dim light shining from our headlamps: we had almost been eaten by an appallingly cute, annoyingly friendly golden retriever out for a late-night walk with its favourite human.

A mix of utter shock, relief and then embarrassment struck me, the pitiful echoes of the angry grizzly bear I'd been impersonating only moments before still hanging awkwardly in the darkness. Clearly confused, a woman continued uncertainly toward us, then shuffled by with a meek "Hi" as she and "the beast" continued on their way.

Five minutes more and we were there, at the end of the trail, laughing nervously under a streetlight with the warm lights of the Banff Springs Hotel welcoming us back to civilization.

That was the last time Amy and I skied the Goat Creek Trail together. She says that fact has more to do with her fear of being strapped down to a makeshift sled than it does with her fear of being eaten. Sure, whatever you say, Amy.

FROZEN REDEMPTION

Margo Talbot

The man who picked me up on the side of the highway just outside of Calgary was about the same age as me, so conversation came easy. I had left Halifax two weeks earlier and was making my way across the country. I was on the run. My goal was to find a job in Vancouver and stay there for the summer. Instead, I ended up finding my destiny the way most of us do: by a random act of the universe.

As we drove through the Bow Valley, Sean explained that he was on his way to Jasper, "so I can drop you off at the junction to the Icefields Parkway. Or you could come north with me..." It was a fork in the road, and I had 45 minutes to decide if I would stay on Highway 1 and continue on to Vancouver or take the detour up through Jasper.

By the time we hit the parkway it was almost dark, and the thought of spending another night in my sleeping bag on the side of the highway lost out to the prospect of heading north with Sean. He had friends in Jasper, so when we arrived after dark we drank a few beers with them and went to sleep on makeshift beds on the floor.

I was the first to wake in the morning and went outside so as not to rouse the others. Within moments of leaving the building, I was struck silent and immobile as I drank in the scene before me. Everywhere I looked there were mountains, rugged beacons of strength and beauty, things I believed I did not possess. My heart felt expansive, in a way it had never felt before, like I was opening up, blossoming. What I didn't know, because I had never felt it, was that for the first time in my life I felt love.

I grew up in a small New Brunswick town, with parents who had no idea how ill-equipped they would be at raising five children. My mother never had a childhood, having raised her nine younger siblings after her mother fell into deep depression while she was still in grade school. My father grew up in one of the notorious Catholic orphanages, where he suffered abuse and neglect at the hands of the priests and nuns. Like me when I hitchhiked out west, my parents thought they could outrun the trauma from their pasts.

Jasper became my home for the next ten years, during which time I would discover the twin forces of the mountain sports that would sustain my hope and the debilitating depression that would strip it away. Outwardly, I could not have been living in a more beautiful place, while inwardly I felt as though I were dying.

As children, we are not equipped to deal with trauma,

so we develop coping mechanisms to survive. Over time, these coping mechanisms become personality traits, eventually outliving the circumstances they were intended to help us navigate. In the end, it is not the actual trauma that debilitates us the most but the disconnection from ourselves that occurs as a result of trying to compartmentalize the emotional distress.

That people have sought the solace of wild places to heal their spirits is not a new concept. Mountains, oceans and deserts have all played a huge part in the myths and dramas of human history. Wild places connect us with that part of ourselves that is inseparable from the power of the universe, a power so artfully reflected in the forces of nature.

Ten years after landing in Jasper, I realized I had grown as much as I possibly could, and that it was time to move on. Although I had created the only stability I had ever known in that town, I had also created a reputation for myself that I was finding impossible to transcend. I came to the Bow Valley to escape the town I had grown to love, the darkness whose depths I plumbed there and the drugs I had come to rely on. I brought with me a truck full of possessions and a criminal record for narcotics trafficking. The little mining town I had passed through ten years earlier, with its glorious mountain backdrop and population base that would afford me a bit of anonymity, became my new home.

Imagine this valley upon my arrival: straight and wide, the weather blows right through it. It gave me the feeling that things were moving in the world and in my life. From the outside, it probably just looked like I was running away again, but it also felt like this could be a fresh start in a new place, where nobody knew anything about me, or my past.

There is a healthy mix of old-time miners and their families, and the people who live here for the access to the mountain sports that they base their lives around. I had come to be a part of this latter group, a group that did not do drugs and was not weighed down by the oppressive forces of their pain. In time, I felt lighter and breathed easier. I was away from the easy access to drugs that I had created in Jasper, as well as the dysfunctional peer group that continually tried to pull me back into that world. There were more job opportunities in Canmore and new friends to be made. I was 30, and for the first time in my life I felt hope for my future.

The impulse to direct our life force into physical expression is as primal as it is universal. The decade I spent in Jasper saw me act out my self-destructive tendencies to the point where my life was best described as a downward spiral. By the time I moved to Canmore the poles had shifted, all because of a fringe activity that most people at that time didn't even know existed.

Two years before leaving Jasper, I had been introduced to the world of ice climbing, a sport where we strap crampons to our boots and swing sharp axe-like tools into frozen waterfalls. During that climb I experienced joy without the use of street drugs for the first time in my life. From that day forward I had something to pour my life energy into that was as creative as it was fun. Until I swung my first tool – essentially a long shaft with a sharp pick on the end – into the ice, I thought that happiness was for other people, people whose pasts weren't heavy enough to keep their dreams forever grounded. Until I climbed my first frozen waterfall, I had no idea that a single activity could turn the landscape of my life from desolation and despair into the pursuit of passion.

Four months after moving to Canmore, my third ice climbing season was upon me. It was late October, and the classic one-pitch climb formed a sheet of ice pasted on a cliff band partway up Ranger Creek in Kananaskis Country. I was with Karen, a newfound friend and climbing partner. We stood protected at the base of the climb, while all around us were slopes that would soon become avalanche-prone as the snow began to fall in earnest. As I flaked out the ropes, Karen offered me the lead. I clipped the gear to my harness and started up.

It is always the same for me: as soon as I swing my axe into the ice, calm sweeps over me. No sooner do I take my first step off the ground than I find peace in the rhythmic sound of metal hitting ice. Ice climbing has enough inherent danger, and requires so much focus, that when I am on the ice I am brought into the present moment. The smooth surface becomes an extension of my body, becomes my vertical support system. The world falls away as my otherwise scattered mind becomes laser-focused on the task at hand.

About ten metres up, I hung from my left tool as I placed my first piece of protection into the ice. As I clipped the ropes into the screw, Karen told me what a great job I was doing. I looked down at her and smiled, appreciative of her support. I continued to work my way up the climb, twisting my ice screws into the holes created by other climbers to make things easier. I attached a sling to each screw that I placed, clipping one end of the nylon to the screw and the other end to my rope. Before I knew it, I was at the top of the climb. I clipped into the bolted belay on the rock wall up and to the right of where the ice ended.

I pulled up the slack in the rope and put Karen on belay. As she climbed, I looked out across the valley, taking in the strength and beauty of the peaks that surrounded me. I felt large inside, expanded, the way I always have in the mountains. Climbing gives me something I never thought possible: a sense of peace.

In the mountains we come home to ourselves. Simply by being in the landscape, another dimension opens up inside of us. There is a feeling of transcendence, of being on a holiday from the day-to-day affairs of life. The space this creates within the architecture of the psyche will become crucial over the next decade of my journey.

As we hiked back down to the truck, I felt the pieces of my life searching for me, threatening to infiltrate my peaceful state of mind. My weekly appointment with the psychologist was just two days away, and for one hour we would continue the process of unearthing the broken shards and piecing together the mosaic of my life. Although climbing feels like another addiction to me, I intrinsically know that it is only a matter of time before I can transpose the feeling of peace and presence into other areas of my life.

Climbing and therapy are the new twin forces of my life and are inner and outer reflections of each other. In both worlds, I am called to face challenges that stretch the limits of what I think I can do, and who I believe I can become. I feel myself moving closer to my potential, one session, and one frozen waterfall, at a time. Both worlds hold the key to the most potent drive humans possess: that of connecting with our life force, which is the fundamental power of the universe.

SEARCHING FOR THE BOW VALLEY'S OLDEST TREE

Dustin Lynx

As I locked the vehicle and approached the obscure trail-head, I wondered if the tree I had in mind could surpass the current record of 700 years held by a Douglas fir near Banff. I found the faint start of the trail tucked behind a road sign, a yellow declaration of a curvy road ahead.

Though I clearly remembered that it was a white-bark pine, I couldn't quite remember its size. That's why I packed an exotic tool used by forestry workers called an increment bore. This particular one was longer than most, blue and had orange flagging tape streaming from one end with my friend's name clearly written in Sharpie. He had showed me how to use it properly and made me swear an oath to return it in good condition. It was his favourite one, he explained.

The whitebark pine is a relative newcomer to North

America; it arrived less than two million years ago. The species originated in Asia, and, like humans, it crossed Berengia, the land bridge that existed until recent geologic times in the north Pacific. Its habitat now covers the western mountain ranges from Alaska to southern California and the adjacent Rocky Mountains. According to the "Bible" – Ben Gadd's *Handbook of the Canadian Rockies* – this species is unlikely to reach as old an age as the Doug-fir he cites as the Bow Valley's record holder, because they live in such hostile environments and tend to rot from the inside out. Undeterred, I set off, knowing that the one I had in mind was a contender nonetheless.

I must admit that the whitebark is one of my favourite tree species. It's a mountain tree that favours open, craggy places where rock meets sky. Whether atop a high mountain crest such as Yamnuska or a spiny hogback in nearby Bow Valley Provincial Park, these trees take root at the very same places that I find to be interesting vantages. Because of their airy perches, the wind shapes them into some of the most unexpected forms, from ground-hugging shrubs to twisted poles that are mostly dead – save for a narrow path of living bark corkscrewing its way to a single live branch. They can have a single trunk or be multistemmed, but the thing that really hooked me about this tree is how it gets to these rocky viewpoints.

Pinus albicaulis (the Latin name for whitebark pine) produces fist-sized cones containing one of the richest food sources anywhere, the pine nut. Think of the ones you've enjoyed in expensive salads. They can grow as long as a fingernail and have as many calories and as much fat as chocolate truffles. One of the dozens of animals that favour this food is a plain-looking grey bird about the size of a jay. It has a black, rapier-like bill about as long as your pinkie finger and is called the Clark's nutcracker. It has a mutualistic relationship with the whitebark: they depend on each other, the bird for its sustenance and the tree for its propagation. This bird is one of the only animals that can open the otherwise impenetrable cones. It collects the nuts in a pouch under its tongue – up to 125 at a time – and caches them in open areas at treeline, a beak-length under the soil, up to 35 kilometres away. The forgotten or neglected hoards happen to be planted in just the right conditions for the next generation of whitebark to start growing. The real limiting factor inhibiting the rate of habitat expansion is that the whitebark takes up to 50 years to reach maturity and start producing cones.

Before I could adjust my backpack and hit the trail, a sleek silver car pulled up and the passenger window slid down. "What's up this road?" asked the driver.

"The trailheads for Goat Creek and Ha Ling," I said.

"Is there something nice to see?" she pressed.

"There's a pullout with a nice view of the valley," I ventured. The window slid up and she drove on. I wondered how her low-slung car would handle the washboard of the Smith-Dorrien road and if she would later regret her sightseeing trip. I couldn't blame her for trying. There are only a few places in the Bow Valley where visitors can drive up to a viewpoint, if you include Mount Norquay and the Moraine Lake Road further west. I suppose I was after "something nice to see" as much as anyone.

I crested the first steep hill and had to stop to catch my breath. In front of me was a jumble of fallen lodgepole pine trees across the trail. They looked like they had been freshly knocked over and probably didn't even know they were uprooted yet. The lofty ridgeline on the East End of Rundle – known affectionately as EEOR by locals, like the character from the Winnie-the-Pooh stories – can focus wind into a powerful battering ram that can knock down a healthy stand of trees in seconds. I negotiated my way around and walked through several dry spiderwebs, which seem to only appear at face level on my hikes. Being over six feet tall, I guessed that others walk below them, but I couldn't imagine many hikers on this trail.

Thanks to some flagging tape marking the way, it didn't take me long to reach the trail junction I was looking for. It would take me up one of EEOR's forested ridges to the hanging valley behind the massive cliffs visible from Canmore. I looked at my altimeter, which read 1700 metres, about 200 metres higher than the trailhead and, incidentally, 400 metres above my home, near downtown Canmore, which I could see clearly beyond the Nordic Centre.

I continued on to the bedrock of the drainage after nearly missing a second trail junction off the ridge. The flagging tape I noticed along the way vanished, like the trail, in a few steps. No worry. I could see the grove of whitebark above a pockmarked cliff, the centre of which was overhanging where water and other debris would flow during the spring melt. I looked for the ledge system that I'd followed many years ago. Instead I spied a wisp of a trail linking ledges and ramps that I had to climb hand over hand in parts. How the goats and sheep managed it, I didn't know.

Having reached the top of the dry waterfall, I turned around and looked over the precipice. I could see the swaths of forest wiped neatly away by avalanches that freight-train down the ephemeral creek each year. I resumed my hike and quickly reached the first of the whitebark pines, also known as the "creeping" pine. This specimen, which I touched with reverence, was ten metres tall, except that it was growing downhill, parallel to the ground. I climbed past its roots, uphill. I was in disbelief even though I could touch the evidence with my own hand; this was the only mature tree growing in the drainage. All the other trees kept a healthy distance up the banks and away from the annual carnage – or from garbage. It occurred to me that I was standing in EEOR's garbage chute, where the mountain's waste was carried away in the form of fractured rock, dirt and water in all its states. Even the air drained down this V-shaped valley.

A solid, cold wind gathered and poured past me. At 2000 metres now, I could see Mount Rundle's long crest directly above me and I could tell that rain was on its way. Not wanting to get turned around by nasty weather, I immediately began searching for the largest of the whitebarks.

Sooner than expected, I spotted the tree that I was looking for. It was unmistakable, a massive trunk that split into two at eye level and continued up to a massive canopy, reaching 20 metres tall. I wanted to get right to work, but an urge to explore carried me higher, to 2100 metres, until I was sitting on the talus next to a sapling, barely a metre tall. It sat on the treeline, above which there are no forests, only a scant few outposts of trees huddled and stooped amidst the forbidding elements.

I studied the young whitebark pine at my feet. The species is named for the powdery white bark that occurs on the immature trees, becoming duller and then scaly with age. Putting a hand on the tree, I could bend it right over until it touched the ground and let it spring up again. They are incredibly flexible. Their branches don't break, they only bend. However, looking downslope, I saw plenty of stumps, the only remaining parts of mature individuals ripped away by snow avalanches. On the sapling, I counted eight gouges, probably from rockfall. Looking more closely at the grove as a whole, I could see that branches tended to grow on the downhill portion of the trees, away from the wind and the falling debris. And in the background, I could see Canmore. What a resolute species to grow so far up the mountain, away from the comparatively lush valley bottom.

Much of the Bow Valley flooded in 2013. Water rose under the foundations of my home for the first time. Friends had their basements flooded and even their foundations eroded away by the surging Cougar Creek. We were lucky. It could have been much worse, considering the fact that we had built so many homes on the shifting gravel of alluvial fans. I realized, sitting there, that this patch of whitebark pine does so much to mitigate the severity of those flood events. The shade from their canopies keeps snow from melting too rapidly, and the roots hold on to soil that would otherwise wash downhill into the Bow River, 700 metres below. They are the Bow Valley's first line of defense, a natural safety net so unlike the steel cable and concrete monstrosity placed at the mouth of Cougar Canyon after the floods.

Water has always shaped the Bow Valley. I imagined the glaciers that occupied this part of the world for the better part of the last two million years, and it occurred to me that when the glaciers retreated about 15,000 years ago, the treeline would have been at the valley's bottom. Enterprising Clark's nutcrackers would have found moraine and other freshly uncovered ground, planting generations of whitebark pine that, in turn, would have pioneered the way for other trees, plants, fish and even us. The earliest human artifacts from this area are found at the bottom of Lake Minnewanka, a 13,000-year-old campsite. It's possible the people were just sightseeing, but they were likely hunting.

Droplets of water like sea spray reached me from the other side of Rundle, forced up and over the massive ramp by the approaching storm. I decided to cut across the top of the grove and then downhill. On the way, I stopped at a whitebark that measured 1.5 metres in circumference at the height of my sternum. I marvelled at the ease of using the increment bore. With only a few effortless twists, it cored its way through years of growth rings into the pith, the very centre of the tree. I stowed the sample in a section of my hiking pole so that it wouldn't get damaged before I had a chance to count all the lines of the tubular sample, about 30 centimetres long, damp and aromatic.

Continuing down to the tree that I'd come to sample in the first place, I slipped on some loose rock and painfully rode on my backside until I got my footing again. I laughed and remembered a friend saying that adventure, really, is dealing with the unexpected: precipitous goat trails, big floods and even washboard roads. In this light, whitebarks are the true adventurers of the Bow Valley.

I felt like an intruder when I finally reached the tree. Standing there with the increment bore, I put my hand on the fine scales of bark as a sign of gratitude and respect before I drilled into it. I imagined how much longer the sample from this tree would be than the first, but as I turned the handles of the bore, I felt the resistance dramatically lessen. Beyond the outer ten centimetres, the trunk felt hollow. I tried another spot, a bit higher on the other side of the tree, with the same result. The core that I pulled out disintegrated in my hands. Sawdust. Before leaving, I wrapped my measuring tape around the trunk and found out that it was 3.5 metres. Astonishing!

On the return trip, it occurred to me that I hadn't seen a single Clark's nutcracker during my hike. Perhaps they had already plundered all the pine nuts from the enticing cones that these trees hold skyward for them. Their absence reminded me that the whitebark pine is in serious decline throughout its range. A fungal disease called blister rust, introduced to North America over a century ago, targets these trees, and outbreaks of mountain pine beetle can decimate an entire grove in a season, leaving an eerie "ghost forest" of standing deadwood bleaching in the sun like so many bones. Nearby, Banff National Park has a program to replant this keystone species in areas affected the most.

Back in my kitchen, I pulled the single core sample from my hiking pole. I counted just under 300 lines with the help of a magnifying glass and good light. The gaps between the lines were five times denser than the sample I had taken from a spruce tree in my front yard the previous week. Extrapolating the growth ring count and circumference, I estimated that the larger tree with the 3.5-metre circumference would be at least 800 years old. Though I can't prove its age definitively, I'm delighted. This tree is one of the oldest in the Bow Valley, but I didn't really need a special tool to appreciate the whitebark pine – age is only one of its fascinating characteristics. Instead, I feel that I was called, as if by the voice of an Elder, to literally see my home not from a drive-up viewpoint but from a compassionate seat beside one of the Bow Valley's older inhabitants.

HIGH PEAKS AND
DEEP ROOTS

Barry Blanchard

The con-mobile sputtered to a halt in the Muleshoe picnic area on the old Banff-to-Laggan (Lake Louise) coach road. Construction of the road began in 1911, and it was largely built on the backs of Ukrainian internees who had been rounded up nationwide under the War Measures Act of the First World War. The men were tented during the summer in a concentration camp below Castle Mountain, 32 kilometres to the north.

Phil stepped from the driver's side, wearing a green and brown plaid shirt, brown corduroy knickers and green wool knee-length socks. He had a red bandana tied around his neck. It was important to Phil to look like a climber. I wore blue jean painter's pants and a white Santa Cruz Skateboards T-shirt. I dearly would have liked to look like a climber, but I couldn't afford it. Phil, my girlfriend Jamie, a number of my high-school buddies and I all had part-time jobs at Sport Chek, Calgary's first big-box sports retailer. Phil had worked there longer and helped me get my job in the tennis and fledgling skateboard departments. Hard to believe that part of my job was to rocket around the perimeter of the parking lot on Saturday afternoons on Calgary's sole motorized skateboard. All of my paycheques were being spent on basic climbing equipment and partying, and I hadn't got to the point of considering climbing clothing.

"How many do you think there are?" I asked.

"Looks like at least a half-dozen."

In a gravel flat in the Bow River far below us, and close to the truncated oxbow that looked like a mule shoe and gave the area its name, a cluster of black bears were milling about in the sun.

"Shit, you don't think that they'll come up here, do you?" I asked.

"I don't know. I hope not. Let's go up there," Phil said, pointing to the southwest face of Mount Cory, high above the other side of the highway.

Plate upon plate of sedimentary limestone scraped upwards, looking like a massive deck of tarot cards that had been dragged backwards so that half of the face of each of a half-dozen cards was exposed and stacked onto the next card, the next fortune. The strata lay to the same incline as Wasootch Slabs, but for 1,000 feet – ten times the height of my previous climbs. The most-identified cave entrance in the Canadian Rockies – the Hole In The Wall – sat low and right on the face, and my eyes, and curiosity, were pulled into the deep black of the portal – a gateway to the underworld. For as long as humans have inhabited the Bow Valley, they have hiked up to see what is there – 11,000 years of finding sheep shit and a pinch-off 30 metres in. A single crack split the left side of the face from bottom to top. The most obvious rock climbing line in the valley, Cory Crack.

In 1960 Hans Gmoser was a hard-working Canadian mountain guide who had emigrated from Austria in 1951. His client that day was Jack Mackenzie, a successful Calgary businessman who would soon partner with Hans to create the new venture of heli-skiing. Hans went on to become the most financially accomplished mountain guide in the history of our profession. Eventually I, too, would become a mountain guide and go on to serve on Hans's executive during his presidency of the Association of Canadian Mountain Guides in the mid-'90s. Hans was in his early 60s at the time, and I was amazed by his work ethic and discipline. I received numerous emails from him time-stamped between one and three in the morning. Of he and Jack Mackenzie's first ascent of Cory Crack, Hans wrote: "It was one of the most enjoyable rock climbs that I have ever done. The rock was as solid as concrete and from the top it was an easy walk back to the highway."

Meanwhile, rain had weathered the limestone to grey, and it was clean and pleated with inch-deep runnels that reminded me of the skin of a giant cactus, but not leathery or spiny – the edges of the crack felt as hard as marble. At the crux the crack necked down to eight inches, and it was vertical and as compact as poured concrete that had been polished. A dead tree was locked into the crack above me, bone dry and ash grey, like an elephant's femur baked in the sun of the savanna; above it a basin of scree and talus was held in check. Getting by the bone tree felt like wrestling an opponent who was twice my size and immovable. I resorted to swarming, and I was a wreck when I teetered into the pool of loose rock, a volley of which clattered off toward Phil.

"Fuck, Blanch! Take it easy up there, man." His shouts wafted up to me on a cloud of gravel dust.

On a sitting hip belay, I brought up Phil then continued on to lead all of the pitches. I seemed to be able to figure things out better than Phil, hang on through the long minutes of desperation and mounting panic as I groped for holds and committed to faith, jerking from point of balance to point of balance, all the while mimicking the techniques I'd read about, working to make my protection placements look like what I'd seen in books.

We tromped back into the Muleshoe parking lot. In 2006 Hans Gmoser fell from his road bike here and became a quadriplegic. A man of iron-cast will, he chose to pull the plug two days later, after nodding goodbye to his wife and two sons. Cory Crack bore witness to his crash. We now call it the Gmoser Crack.

Two months after Phil's and my ascent, I borrowed my Aunt Joanne's mustard-coloured 1976 Toyota Corolla and drove off to the Muleshoe parking lot to sleep in the car. Any sound snapped me upright to wipe my condensed breath from the passenger's side window and peer out into the night. I was sleeping nervously against the edge of two things that I wasn't supposed to be doing. The first was sleeping in the car, which must have been against some regulation or other, the second was that I was planning to solo Cory Crack the next day, and I'd only been climbing for six months. Then I sank into a deeper sleep and didn't wake until I felt the humid heat of the morning sun cutting into the Toyota and steaming off the condensation and making it feel like a greenhouse.

I was up the route in an hour and a half. The climbing commanded all of my concentration and I felt in control. It felt good to correct the mistakes that Phil and I had made, and I felt a glow of competency and pride in the accomplishment. Interestingly, I would not solo again for a couple of years and it would be a decade, and several thousand days of climbing down the road, before I really did a lot of it. On Cory Crack I was much more interested in trying to get better, to become a real climber. Climbing without a rope at lower grades didn't hold as much attraction as pushing my envelope on the sharp end of the rope.

^ ^ ^

A funnel of frost-shattered shale marks the top of the Calgary Route on Mount Yamnuska. The mountain's name is a Stoney word that translates to "sheer cliff face," and that is apt because some of the routes are over 300 metres long, engirding bold 100-metre sweeps of overhangs that back into space for metres. To see the copper tint of the early-morning sun glow across the mile-wide width of the south face is to see its climbing lines revealed and radiating like polished tiger eye. Mark, a guy I know from the Stoney Reservation, has been trying to teach me the proper pronunciation for over ten years and I'm getting closer – EE-yem-a-NUSHK-a – but I'm still not there. Mark's black braids hang to his waist. "I've seen over 40 winters, brother, and I've never cut my hair. I still have my baby hair." He handed me the piece of paper that he'd printed the phonetic pronunciation onto. I tried again.

"Close; not bad for a half-breed."

"Can I keep this?"

He snatched the paper from my hands. "This?" He held it between us like a business card. "This isn't knowing." And he crumpled it into his palm and turned and walked away. Tough love between us First Nations people.

On top of the Calgary Route, hard-edged tawny fragments of shale the size of a deck of cards lie in file, looking like they've been raked. Gravity funnels them to fall, in time, into the 2.5-foot-wide abysmally black crack that is the final squeeze of the route. Shoulders of water-washed Precambrian limestone jut out from the dark slot; precipitation and wind have swept the rock clean like an archaeologist's brush revealing a chisel-cut corner of marble. I've passed the place a half-dozen times a year, walking down the gentle backside descent trail. I forever see myself huddled into the swale or the funnel hypothermic and hallucinating at two a.m. on a late-October morning in 1977. I was 18 and holding fast to a sit-anchored hip belay, my partner Gray's full body weight cutting the rope into me, deepening the dark ring of bruises that semicircled my waist like the lash-marks of a whip.

Gray Dickson worked in the shoe department at Sport Chek. He was reserved and quiet compared to most of my friends, and he lived with his spinster mother. Gray was her only child, and the one time I met her, in her house, I could feel the legacy of Great Britain in the tea and crumpets. Gray had done what I dreamed of doing – climbed several routes on Mount Yamnuska. It was where the heroes from my hometown, Calgary, climbed – Brian Greenwood, Urs Kallen, Jim Elzinga and, foremost, John Lauchlan. I'd seen several of John's slideshows about climbing in the St. Elias and even effused congratulatory ravings at him after he returned from the south face of Mount Logan. He was intense and gracious and fully aware of the fact that I didn't have a damn clue. I knew as much about the greater ranges as I did the headwaters of the Amazon – the river was wet, the mountains were snowy.

Gray and I decided to attempt the Calgary Route, which Hans Gmoser and his lifelong friend and climbing partner, Franz Dopf, put up in 1953. I borrowed my Uncle Ken's 1959 Plymouth Fury station wagon. It had sat in a barn for a decade before he bought it from the farmer for a hundred bucks. It had started first turn, had foot-high tail fins and push-button "TorqueFlite" gearshifts on the dash. Gray and I had just enough cash between us to fill it with gas. It rumbled into the old Yam parking lot low and heavy like a slow-moving tank.

The fallen leaves had aged from gold to mottled brown; they crackled under my feet. Bark peeled in curls from the trunks of the aspens, and it looked like papyrus but crumpled like the skin of a wasp's nest when I pulled on the tissue-thin sheets. Skeletal branches reached into the cold morning air. The foothills had long since turned to brown, and there had been a frost overnight. Once Gray got us onto the approach trail, I charged, red-lining my pulse well over 200 beats per minute, and marched on double time, head bobbing, until sweat was weeping from my chest and my lungs raged. The morning sun was touching the top of the wall and washing it copper. I was so excited. "Hurry up, Gray," I chanted to myself as I bent at the waist, shifting the weight of my pack off my shoulders and onto my flattened back. I braced my hands to bent knees and breathed hard, waiting for Gray.

I led every pitch, and we were doing okay until we entered the squeeze chimney that forms the top four rope-lengths of the route. I fought. Knees pressed to stone, elbows paddling backwards over black rock and bracing the bones of my forearm, like a wooden truss in a mine shaft, against the flattened flesh of my palms, my fingers fanned out and pasted down the wall. I'd gain centimetres by squirming my shoulder blades and scraping my back up while torquing tension onto my elbows, palms, the backs of my hips, my splayed-out knees and the backwards- and downward-thrusting soles of my feet. It was sick. My chest would get wedged and I'd panic and thrash to free it, to breathe. I'd start to slip and I'd push harder, stapling the imprint of the rock's surface into blanched skin. I felt like a bullfrog in bondage. Every so often I would find an in-cut hold and brace a heel onto it and rest and breathe and try to rationalize the arc of the ropes hanging from my harness and disappearing into the darkness like lines dropping into a deep dark well. "How much farther until I find some pro?"

Gray couldn't climb the chimney.

"Keep the rope TIGHT!" he wailed. A current of bewildered fear crackled on his words like radio static and then he fell and the rope ratcheted hard on my waist and my body went rigid. I was scraped downward six inches toward the coal chute of the crack. He fell five more times, and then just sat on the cable-taut rope for ten minutes. The pressure parted the subcutaneous fat over my left hip and the rope burned down onto the bone.

"GRAY! What the fuck are you doing?"

"I can't fucking do this!" His reserved manner was gone and he sounded like a grade school kid on the verge of tears, and that just made me madder.

"You fucking HAVE to do it! We can't get down from here!" I'd never done a 500-foot retreat and neither had he. The walls around me seemed to close in.

"Can you hold the green rope tight?" Gray shouted.

"Yes." And I wrapped it around my waist with my left hand while holding Gray's belay with my right.

"Okay! The green rope is okay."

"Are you sure?" More fear.

"Yes! I'm fucking sure. Yes!"

The pressure shifted from the brown rope onto the green. Two hours later, Gray pulled onto my stance. He'd ascended the ropes by tying an overhand knot into one, stepping his weight into it, and then tying a higher overhand in the other and stepping up into it. Soon the chains of knots were jamming below him and he had to step down and untie them to clear them. He kept himself safeguarded – always – by clipping slings from his harness into both of the overhands that he was working with. I sat braced against the walls, holding his body weight, and then I would lead. Anxiety waxed on the waning sun.

"Can you see the top?" Gray pleaded.

"No, there's more."

Darkness. The absolute dark of night in the bowls of the crack, a surreal slice of starlight and the night sky, cut and defined by the outer walls like a door cracked open to faint and distant candlelight. I led by feel, and by the faint blue illumination from the sparkling of static electricity as my positively charged clothing scraped over the grounded rock. A new form of fear within me – the real night-fear of the unknown, my honest doubt as to whether we would survive. I ended the pitches where I could brace my body and hold Gray. He took three times as long to climb the pitches as I did. The rope bit deeper. I began to hate him for not being able to suck it up and fight for the chimneys, to deal. When I came onto the ammo box with the route register in it, I signed my name in by starlight and feel and I didn't sign Gray in.

At two a.m., I slapped my cold and swollen hands onto the water-washed limestone shoulders at the top of the route. I pressed up and staggered into the funnel and swale of broken shale. I'd eaten the last of my food, a box of Smarties, at noon the day before, washed them down with the last of my water. I sat down and braced myself and shouted to Gray to start, and then I suffered.

A cold wind out of the west swirled into the funnel and bit. Spasms of violent shivering rattled my skeleton every four minutes. I'd clench my eyes shut and blather prayers. I made a number of promises to God that I would go on to break. My hallucinations were magnificent. The headlights of the sparse traffic and the lights from the houses on the Stoney Reservation became a massive space complex like something out of *Star Wars*. I watched a bear amble by me, could hear his breathing. A neon orange sign spun at me from the horizon like a zooming shot of a newspaper in a movie clip, VOTE ROSS ALGER, in bold black capital letters. A procession of bowed supplicants walking upwards in a torchlit line, their heads hooded in burlap swaddle. I prayed in time to their murmured chanting. I prayed to survive.

Gray arrived. For hours we grouped and stumbled down the descent trail, down the scree. I wore through my fingerless Miller gloves sitting on my ass and easing down the scree on locked arms and dug-in heels. Toward treeline we began to catch glimpses of headlights darting up and down the road to the parking lot, red and blue flashers.

"CLIMBERS ON THE MOUNTAIN!" echoing from the cruiser's PA.

By nine p.m. the night before, my mother had become frantic with worry. She called Gray's mother, then she called the Calgary city police, the RCMP, the fire department and the Banff wardens. Basically, anybody with a hat got a call. Soon the Calgary Mountain Rescue Group called her. John Lauchlan had to put down his beer and leave the party he was at.

Dawn came slowly. I finally found the road and fell from the forest into the ditch. I was totally fucked, shattered. I stood slowly and shouted back to Gray. He tumbled out of the forest just as the RCMP cruiser charged to us and ground to a stop, wheels locked, dust swirling. I folded back onto my ass in the ditch.

"You two are in a whole lot of shit," was what the officer bellowed, stepping from the driver's side. But then Don Forrest, the leader of the Mountain Rescue Group, was there and he barged in front of the Mountie and squatted down on his haunches and looked me in the eye and kindly asked, "How are you boys?"

"I'm thirsty. I'm really thirsty."

John Lauchlan thumped his pack down beside Don. Nothing dangled from the outside of the pack. John had on Galibier Super Guide mountain boots, grey knickers and a Peter Storm sweater. I felt like a fake in my battered blue jeans. He handed me a red aluminum water bottle with a wired stopper. I sprung the stopper and greedily guzzled half, then handed it to Gray, who was talking with Don and the Mountie. John's intense blue eyes bore into me from behind his teardrop glasses. I shifted my gaze to the dirt between my feet and then raised it to meet John's.

"I'm sorry for making you be here, man," I said.

He smiled, and told me that he had done the exact same thing on the Grillmair Chimneys route once upon a time.

"No shit?" I asked.

"No shit."

Gray fell into a coma in the passenger's seat. At Scott

Lake Hill, the Trans-Canada Highway gains about 700 feet of elevation. As I drove, the road ramped up into the sky and the foothills fell away and cypress trees lined the shoulders. I blinked and shook my head side to side, but the hallucination persisted. I kept the Fury between the cypress trees, and then the road rounded to horizontal and the cypress trees dissolved into evergreens and I could see the gas station at the top of Scott Lake Hill.

Gray's mother came down the sidewalk to meet him. She put her arm around his shoulder and shepherded him into the house. When I got home, my mother made sure that I was okay and then she fed me. Delicious warm brown bread rolls completely enveloping ground beef and, after a half-dozen of those, white ones stuffed with cherry pie filling. They were one of my favourite things that my mom made. She'd buy the dough premade and frozen and, as I sat at our kitchen table in Gladstone Park that morning, I remembered how she'd told me that she had gotten bored carrying me in her ninth month of pregnancy, when she was 19, and taken to bouncing down the stairs on her butt to get me out. I would be 19 in five months' time. I climbed the stairs to my bedroom slowly. I slept for 18 hours.

It was Monday. I skipped my university classes and spent a lot of the day on the couch. I drank a lot and ate as only a young man can eat: 8,000 calories, as if it was one. A soft light effused my world. Everything looked like the scenes in *Star Trek* when a beautiful woman's face is zoomed into portrait and wreathed in a halo of glow that radiates to the four corners of the TV screen. I felt light, good and slow. The Calgary Route had been, by far, the most intense experience of my life, but I'd promised God that if he just got me down from it I'd never go back up there again. Now I wanted to return; climbing was calling to me.

TRIBUTARIES

Graeme Pole

Older than the mountains is the river that carved the
Bow Valley. Those who explain the genesis and transformation of landscapes – geomorphologists – have
made this pronouncement. They point to two bends in
the Bow River's course – one just west of Banff town,
the other in the gap at the mountain front. At both, the
Bow River hooks a right angle across the grain of the
Front Ranges. The explanation: the river eroded this unlikely course through the nascent mountains, keeping
pace downwards as geologic forces raised the eastern-
most Canadian Rockies, 85 million years ago.

There have been innumerable transformations in the
landscape since. As mountain creation continued, as
ice-age glaciers ebbed and flowed, as mountainsides col-
lapsed, as humankind arrived, some valleys became entrenched while others were blocked, beheaded, dammed
and diverted. At least one geomorphologist has specu-
lated that today's Bow River occupies the southerly

reach of a mega-valley that commenced at the Columbia Icefield. Subsequent faulting and folding of Earth's crust, augmented by the gouging of Pleistocene glaciations, transformed this alignment, separating it into the North Saskatchewan, the Mistaya and the Bow valleys. Others postulate that an ancient Bow River may have flowed northeast past what is now Banff town, through the Minnewanka and lower Ghost valleys, to the plains. And in another possible arrangement, the Cascade River may have flowed southeast past what is now Banff town as it does today, but as the greater stream, ostensibly receiving the Bow River as a tributary.

Today, the Cascade River, its lower reach profoundly altered by hydroelectric diversion and drawdown, is a tributary of the Bow River. Is this possible rearrangement of the landscape that reverses a river's role from receiver to giver, from dominant to subordinate, from mainstem to tributary, merely a notion in the minds of we latecomers to the land?

Perhaps. However, at any given time, the dominant river is the cornerstone of its landscape. It is the palette on which the chemistry and character of all its tributaries are mixed. The dominant river is a product of, and a subsequent blueprint for, the transformation of the surrounding land, its climate and its species.

Rivers are powerful, beautiful, living and magical. They possess the contradictory abilities to connect places in time and space, and to escape them. The existence of the Bow River, of any river, is an effect of its sources, and a cause of its destination. The relative importance of riverine cause and effect is largely dependent on volume of flow. Few rivers in the world can buck the trend in this regard. Any dominance that a particular river may have held is, in the vaster geological sense, now revealed to be a waning, contradictory, years-long regime of dwindling flows peppered with occasional, headline-grabbing flash floods. The Bow River at Banff has lost 12 per cent of its peak summer volume in the last century, yet the June 2013 flood was the greatest in the watershed in a span almost as long.

Rivers were the original routes of passage in western North America. The valleys became places of settlement and have suffered greatly. This is especially so in the constricted topography of mountains. But everywhere, valleys collect more than water. Their rivers have become sewers, and their peopled floodplains and deltas, scapegoats. In a sense, humankind has become an unwanted tributary; a miasmic junkie injecting chemical concoctions, clinging to the promise of endless higher ground while wasting the lowland veins and arteries that sustain it.

Rivers and the landscapes that they traverse possess a tremendous, life-giving capacity to inspire. Not all concentrations of human energy in a single place produce negative results. The process of becoming acquainted with a riverine landscape – to be blessed with its many inspirations – can be tremendously beneficial for the observer and, perhaps, ultimately, for the observed.

Without consciously intending to, in one July a few decades ago, I spent a disproportionate amount of time exploring the headwaters of the Bow River. Pondering that experience, then and now, leaves me with two ir-reducible impressions: The Bow Valley is a grand, time-less place at its very origin. And because the valley is so ancient a feature, the Bow River, its secondary architect, is a watercourse dominated by its creation, not vice versa.

It was a tremendously fitting act of toponymy when explorer Walter Wilcox named a modest mountain in the upper Bow Valley in 1896. Bow Peak's association with the headwaters of the river is obvious, but it would be illuminating to know whether Wilcox named the mountain before or after he and Robert Barrett climbed it during their epic excursion to Fortress Lake. Illumin-ating, because Bow Peak offers the most instructive of any view of the headwaters of the Bow River. To quote Wilcox: "The botanist, the geologist, and the general lover of science will ... find extensive fields of inquiry open to him on every side." Indeed, Bow Peak's summit view reveals the geological composition and structure of the Bow Valley in fine detail, from quartzite founda-tion to limestone lintel. And in every nook and cranny, in every rockbound cirque, on every shaded lee slope, there is a glacier, or the unmistakable imprint of one.

Today's Bow River follows a course inherited from ancestral ice. Its waters trickle as lifeblood away from glaciers that, in comparison to those of ice-age millen-nia, are stubbed fingers extending from aged, shrivelled hands. Nonetheless, their collective reach is still signifi-cant – you can ski hard for a day and not cross length-wise the complex of icefields and glaciers that are the primary sources of the Bow River. But imagine, 18,000 years ago at the apex of the Late Wisconsin Glaciation, the marathon glacial ski traverse that would have been required to link every glacially fed tributary of the Bow River from Bow Summit to beyond the Kananaskis Valley, where the Bow Valley Glacier surged onto the plains – a straight-line distance of more than 100 kilometres.

I find it difficult to grasp the scale of ice-age glaciation, although I have knocked my boots against evidence of it everywhere. There are touchstones to assist the comprehension. Walter Wilcox's photograph of Mount Balfour's tangle of glaciers and icefalls, taken from Balfour Creek on August 16, 1895, is a favourite. It hangs in my study. There is a chaos of ice in that image, much more extensive than in the contemporary view. By means of that contrast, the photograph provides an inkling of an ice age – a frozen nugget framed for understanding.

I finally reached Balfour Creek a month shy of a century after Wilcox. I kayaked across the perfect early-morning mirror of Hector Lake, an adventure in itself, but one that surely pales with how Wilcox, Bill Peyto and a trail cook, whose name history has forgotten, reached the same spot. It would be deception to say that I understand the tribulations involved in successfully packing a glass-negative camera on horseback along the excuse of a trail in the upper Bow Valley – a jackpot of muskeg and fire-felled snags that Wilcox called "the worst in the mountains." And also in getting those glass negatives back to New England in one piece to be developed. I am grateful to Wilcox for acquiescing to his curiosity and courting hardship; devoting his recreational energy, his expensive and precious vacation time, to such enterprise.

The ice-mantled headwall that dominates the inlet to Hector Lake has changed profoundly, and because of Wilcox's wonderful snapshot, we can assay that change. On my visit in July 1995, Wilcox's vantage point lay submerged midstream in Balfour Creek, the glacial torrent that issues from the combined lobes of the Vulture and Balfour glaciers and the unnamed glaciers on Mount Balfour itself. The meltwater stream did not angle south-to-north as in Wilcox's image; it flowed northeast, directly toward me for a distance of several hundred metres, before curving southeast. The creek was narrower than in Wilcox's day, functions of it having become entrenched, and of its reduced volume – the latter a consequence of the creek's dwindling glacial sources.

In moving as close as possible to Wilcox's perspective, I found myself on the north bank of the creek, whereas Wilcox had taken his photograph on the south bank. There is no vegetation visible on the alluvial flat in Wilcox's view. On my visit, willows, avens and mountain fireweed decorated the rubble – nature's hard-won craft of a century. Mountain goats had beaten a path glacierward along the banks, the multitude of their cloven tracks interspersed here and there with that of a grizzly bear. Did Wilcox see such minutiae, or were his footprints among the first in a landscape that had been icebound only a decade earlier?

In Wilcox's photograph, the splaying terminus of the already retreating glacier is perhaps 800 metres distant. When I observed it, the closest ice was at least twice as far removed. Abandoned stream channels criss-crossed the delta like wrinkles on an aged face.

Is there a wisdom on that face, on the face of any landscape? And can that wisdom be communicated? I think so. The impression of permanence conveyed by the mighty eastern flank of Mount Balfour in Wilcox's photograph – and in my experience a century later – is illusion. Piece by piece, the mountain is crumbling. Mount Balfour was created from sediments and was thrust by monumental forces toward the sky. Although it does not yield its form easily, gravity rules, and Mount Balfour does yield. The meltwater stream at my feet in July 1995 was chalky grey – a liquid mountain. Many more tonnes of Mount Balfour have been carried seaward since.

And what of the disappearing ice? Another cycle of ebb and flow, gain and loss; a balance contingent on factors thoroughly dissected by science, yet beyond complete comprehension. Any arguments still postulated against contemporary global climate change fly in the face of Walter Wilcox's photograph and the climatic background noise of more than a century: no matter what the causes, locally, the mean annual temperature at the latitude of Mount Balfour is 1.5 degrees Celsius greater, and the mean annual snowfall has decreased 50 per cent in that interval.

Evidence obtained from ice cores on the Greenland icecap suggests that the onset and termination of the last ice age, the ultimate episode of the Wisconsin Glaciation, may each have occupied less than a decade. Skeptics might argue that, by comparison, the climatic change to which Mount Balfour's glaciers testify is not profound; it may reflect nothing more than a cyclic short-term climatic response, or an aberration of little enduring consequence. Conversely, the evidence could be interpreted as an indication that the retreat of Mount Balfour's glaciers is a threshold indicator, heralding a precipitous alteration in climate.

If the trend of glacial retreat continues, and especially if it accelerates, the viability of human settlement and activity may be threatened, worldwide. If its wellspring of glacial ice is depleted, the Bow Valley will endure but as a barren cadaver. This is not conjecture. There is evidence nearby in this landscape that conjures the presence of a phantom glacier and of a reach of river that is virtually no more.

The extensive delta on the north shore of Bow Lake is an artifact of another time; the product of another incarnation of the Bow River. The trickle that now meanders through willow plain, wet meadow and ptarmigan thicket from Bow Summit to discharge across this delta into the lake is too feeble to have created the landform. Geomorphologists tell us that a torrent that issued from a glacier in Bow Pass was responsible for transporting the substantial alluvium deposited on the delta. That glacier waned and vanished, probably during the Holocene Climate Optimum (HCO) – a period that featured warmer summers and colder winters than present, particularly in the northern hemisphere. The HCO began about 8,000 years ago and peaked about 5,000 years ago. In that interval, the mean annual temperature in the Rockies may have increased between one and three degrees Celsius. The rate of that temperature change, although much less than that of the past century, spelled oblivion for a glacier that may have been more substantial than some at the headwaters of the Bow River today.

If we were willing to take a lesson from the landscape, we would pause in the uppermost reach of the Bow Valley alongside that remnant stream with Wilcox's image of Mount Balfour in our mind's eye. There, in sight of the Wapta Icefield, an icy domain so distant from, yet so essential to, the routine of our existence, we would listen for the tumult of a ghost river flowing from Bow Pass – an ancestral tributary now vastly diminished in volume and size but growing in importance through time. It has a message for us.

CONCLUSION

LAND OF A THOUSAND FUTURES

Stephen Legault

For millennia people have been imagining this valley. In dreams, along song lines, through vision quests and with the soles of their own two feet, people have come into this deep cleft in the limestone crags of the Rocky Mountains to imagine this landscape and their place in it. More recently, people have travelled up the Bow by horse, by train, by bus or by car. Some have followed this wide green valley to reach the high passes that lead further west; others have stayed and settled and made this place home.

There are a thousand stories that have been told while imagining this place and there are as many futures that lead us forward.

One of those stories is typical of many, and has been on my mind since I first heard it several years ago. It's about a woman I know who works in the gas station I frequent, and her tale is emblematic of many in the valley. She is from the Philippines and moved here four years ago to earn money to send home to her family, including several young children. She works two jobs, starting at seven a.m. and working until three in the afternoon at the gas station, then walking to a fast food restaurant, where she works from four p.m. until late in the evening. Then she takes a cab home to sleep for a few hours and starts the whole procedure over again. Her story is part of the tale of this place and, if we're going to imagine this valley, we have to imagine both the opportunity this place presents and how hard life can be here.

You don't know what you're going to get when you ask a cabal of writers to imagine a place. Everybody's got their own take on what it means to envision a landscape and its people. What I got was often deeply personal, sometimes political, but always drawn from the deepest well of human emotion: the desire to know the place called home and understand ourselves within the context of that relationship.

From the moment I arrived in the Bow Valley, on a spring day in 1992, I knew that this would be home. Like most of the writers in this book, and like many of the inhabitants of this valley, past and present, I've come and gone. The valley has a magnetic hold on many of us, but sometimes the pull weakens and we stray, and sometimes the poles reverse and we are pushed away. Sometimes we are drawn back, and we find ourselves returning after circling for some time, to realize that we've never really left. So it was for me.

I love this place, I love its history and I love its people, but sometimes this valley drives me crazy. Sometimes I think we're trapped between the way things have always been and the way things are, with the way things *could* be piling on top just to make the weight so much harder to bear. The Bow Valley has been at the centre of a nationwide debate over national parks and continent-wide deliberations over conservation, and amid all of the rhetoric the Bow Valley is a lived-in landscape, and its people are trying to practise what we preach. It's a heavy lift sometimes, but it's worth it. The world's eyes are on us, and how we treat the land has resulted in conservation victories far beyond these home ranges. Our debates in the Bow Valley have literally helped make the *world* a better place.

When I first arrived in the Bow I was young, idealistic, opinionated and uncomplicated in my vision for the world and how I thought national parks, and the vast sweep of wilderness that surrounds us here, should be. I was frustrated by the ongoing debate over development in Banff, believing then, as I do now, that Canada's national parks should be part of the effort to protect nature, not to exploit it for private profit. Debate over the development of the Chateau Lake Louise, Banff's three ski areas and the creation of a "skywalk" in Jasper has always been couched in the idea that visitors to the park deserve to have these recreational opportunities. That's simply not true. Visitors aren't pushing for these experiences; the people who profit from them are.

One of the possible futures I imagine for the Bow Valley is that someday – maybe soon – we'll reverse the theme-park mentality that has dominated decision making in Banff National Park for more than a generation and reinvent our relationship with nature. The Rocky Mountains, in all their resplendence, don't need glass-bottomed skywalks or via ferrata courses to provide visitors with a national park experience; what we need is time, and space and silence. My most profound experiences in Banff haven't come from the top of a mountain or somewhere deep in the backcountry – though there have been myriad of those – but while sitting quietly along the bankside of the Bow River, alone and lost in my own thoughts, allowing nature to do its good work on my soul.

That's something that nearly everybody who visits Banff could do. Abandon their cars and the gift shops of Banff Avenue for a few hours and stroll to a quiet place and simply sit and appreciate the stillness.

When I moved from Lake Louise – was moved, more accurately – in the mid-1990s, I wondered if I would ever find peace outside the sanctuary of a national park. I found it, to be sure, and in some ways the quietude was deeper after I left behind the hurly-burly pace of a tourist mecca like Lake Louise.

In the deep grotto of a canyon in the Fairholme Range, I found profound quiet and magic. I visited this place often during the six years I lived in Harvie Heights, right on the boundary of Banff National Park. It became my refuge and part of my inspiration during periods of conflict over the Bow Valley Wildland and other places I was advocating for. In those days, I could imagine many possible futures for the Bow Valley, not all of them positive. The valley's protection became a necessity. Many others shared both my concern and my vision, and together we advocated for a park that could encompass all the stories that made the Bow Valley so important.

Inspired by the Yellowstone to Yukon Conservation Initiative, our dream was to ensure that the Bow Valley would remain part of a functioning wildlife movement corridor that connected the vast mountain landscapes on either side of it, allowing bears, elk, cougars, wolves and others – and the genetic diversity that they represented – to move freely through the confines of an increasingly urban landscape. We knew that even in the vast protected landscapes of the mountain national parks, wildlife would suffer if it wasn't connected to other populations. We envisioned the Bow Valley as a home to wild things and a passageway between even larger storehouses of diversity.

Those opposed? Developers of said valley, boosters for a bigger Canmore and often their cumulative supporters in government.

Two futures clashed: one where the Bow Valley outside of Banff National Park was part of an international vision for conservation and wildlife connectivity, and one where Canmore burst its banks and sprawled up and down the valley, choking off the millennia-old wildlife passage.

In time, the former vision won out, but not without compromise. New parks were created, wildlife movement corridors designated, debated, redrawn and further demarcated. Golf courses and mountain biking trails became acceptable components of these narrow passageways that bordered Canmore and its neighbouring towns.

This vision continues to compete with others that don't accommodate wildlife and wildlands so amicably. Canmore, even with its current (2016) progressive and visionary leadership, is still wedged between high mountain walls and bursting with year-round residents and tens of thousands of visitors on any given weekend. We're all here for the same reason: we love this place. The Bow Valley is singular in its ability to inspire; the ease with which we can wander out of our front doors or away from our hotels and reach the summit of a peak is astonishing.

But we're all here. And as in Banff, that's the problem. None of us are bad people for making the decision to put down roots in this valley, but cumulatively we have an impact.

And we're not alone. I don't know if I'm the only one who finds this paradoxical – I don't think I could be – but the fact that Canmore makes its living by promoting its mountain scenery and recreational amenities, and neighbouring Exshaw makes its way by mining them, feels like a collision of futures.

The rock industry is the elephant in the valley. We all know it's there, can't avoid its obvious impact on the Bow Valley, but so far we don't really talk about it much. Even the conservation community in the Bow Valley has largely steered clear of addressing the massive impact of limestone quarrying, choosing to focus on protecting narrow corridors of land for wildlife movement rather than going toe-to-toe with this industrial powerhouse.

Limestone quarrying and processing is a vital part of the Bow Valley's economy, and not just for the Municipal District of Bighorn. As Ruth Oltmann points out, it's been a part of the community for more than a century. Many employees of the valley's three main mining operations and mills live in Canmore (though more of them are now choosing less-expensive Cochrane), providing a tax base for both the town and the municipal district. LafargeHolcim – the largest of the operations – is one of the most generous sponsors of sports, the arts and community events in the Bow Valley: you'd be hard-pressed to find an event that doesn't bear its logo. During the public debate over the Bow Valley Wildland in the late 1990s, it was a vocal advocate of the park and the protection of wildlife corridors, so long as neither of these ideas impaired its future operations. Today, it is still an advocate for conservation, but with the same provisions.

But the massive rents in the flanks of Loder Peak and Grotto Mountain, and the complete levelling of Door Jamb Mountain (really a shoulder of Grotto), leave me to wonder: How much longer can these two futures share such a small valley? When will the future that says, "We need all the mountains that remain to attract more tourists and provide us with peace" collide with the future that says, "We have to take them apart piece by piece"?

If these competing futures weren't complex enough, add climate change into the conversation.

It's strange that, after I called for essays for this book, nobody else wrote specifically about the floods of 2013, but many of the authors had it as a preoccupation. Bob Sandford touched on it in his fine essay, and Jocey Asnong gave it a colour scheme. Dustin Lynx uncovered hidden secrets revealed by the floodwaters. It's hard to look at the Bow Valley the same way after seeing what 18 hours of hard rain can do.

And for good reason. Dr. John Pomeroy is the Canada Research Chair for Hydrology and Climate Change, a professor at the University of Saskatchewan and a resident of Canmore.

He, like many others, has been warning us about the future of the Bow Valley, and all those who depend on these headwaters for water across prairie Canada, for years. Glaciers make up a very small amount of the water in rivers like the Bow, but they do tend to release their water when it's needed the most – later in the summer. What Dr. Pomeroy warns us of is the great fluctuations that are occurring in when our precipitation falls, and what happens as those changes reverberate across the land.

Add to this the ever-present concern that as these mountain forests – profoundly altered from the time that the First People travelled and hunted in them – are overdue for a massive fire, and the spectre of a changing climate introduces more possible futures that we might care to consider.

And what of it? One of the wonders of living in a place like the Bow is that we have John Pomeroy and Bob Sandford, we have Kevin van Tighem and Harvey

Locke to help us imagine our future. If there is a place on Earth with the intellectual firepower to think and act its way out of the predicament we're in, this is the place. All we need to do is take our future seriously; how hard could that be?

Meanwhile, the valley inspires. The peaks, the woods and the aspen parklands that shelter us and loom large in our everyday provide us with sustenance to live extraordinary lives. The valley breeds exceptional people who strive to be a reflection of this marvellous landscape. May we always find a way to measure ourselves against this place.

ACKNOWLEDGMENTS

The easiest acknowledgment to give for this book is to the pantheon of writers who contributed to it. You have my eternal thanks for your dedication to place, your passion for language and your contribution to a vision.

Anybody who has ever read the dedication section of any of the books penned by these authors knows that behind each of them is a team. Loved ones, spouses, ex-spouses, friends, pets, community: a network of supporters who make it possible for us to write. I extend my gratitude to all of you.

Some of these essays have appeared elsewhere. The late Jon Whyte's "Business of the River" is used by permission from Summerthought Publishing and Postmedia. It originally appeared in the Banff *Crag & Canyon* and was published posthumously in *Mountain Chronicles*, edited by Brian Patton. I am grateful to Mike McIvor for helping select this essay for *Imagine This Valley*.

Kevin Van Tighem's "Bow Corridor: Heart of a Mountain Ecosystem" originally appeared in *Environment Views* magazine and was later included in the collection *Coming West: A Natural History of Home*, published by Altitude.

Ben Gadd's piece, "Yam," was published in *Mountain Heritage Magazine* in 1998, though he penned it for the first effort at *Imagine This Valley* the year before.

"Why We Are So Drawn to the Magnitude and Beauty of Mountains," by Ian Brown, originally appeared in the *Globe and Mail* on April 27, 2013.

"Green Eyes on the Goat Creek Trail," by Kristy Davison, was originally penned for this book but was published in *Highline Magazine* before this publication went to print.

A version of "The History of a Fantasy," by Katherine Govier, originally appeared in the July/August 2012 issue of *Alberta Views*.

Barry Blanchard's essay, "High Peaks and Deep Roots," is excerpted from *The Calling: A Life Rocked by Mountains*, published by Patagonia Books.

I owe friend and contributor Colette Derworiz a special debt of thanks for coming to my rescue to proofread *Imagine This Valley*. It saved my bacon.

"The Great Uncertainty" is a blog entry of mine, posted at StephenLegault.com on June 26, 2013.

Thanks to Jocey Asnong for her help identifying potential contributors from the more than 70 publishing authors who make this valley their home. As always, I am deeply grateful to the support of Café Books, which supports so many of us in so many ways.

Peter Norman has done a masterful job as this book's copy-editor, taking disparate voices from over a 20-year time period and making them sound and read as one.

Lastly, I would like to thank Don Gorman of Rocky Mountain Books, who during a chat over tea in Canmore in 2013 said yes and helped us *Imagine This Valley*.

CONTRIBUTORS

Rob Alexander is a Calgary-based writer, journalist, historian and artist. He grew up in Canmore after moving from Edmonton in 1971 with his parents and his sister. Rob studied writing and photography at Prescott College in Arizona and journalism at Mount Royal University. He worked as a reporter for nearly two years at the *Canmore Leader* newspaper and then spent 13 years at the *Rocky Mountain Outlook* newspaper, often writing about art, culture and the history and heritage of the Bow Valley and the Rocky Mountains. He is the author of *The History of Canmore* and co-author of *Exshaw: The Heart of the Valley* and *The Exshaw Cement Plant: Foundations for the Future*. Even though Rob moved from Canmore to Calgary in 2014 with his wife and daughter, he still freelances for the *Outlook* and other regional publications.

Jocey Asnong was raised by a pack of wild pencil crayons in a house made out of paper and stories. After finishing several years of illustration school at Sheridan College, she left the land of maple trees and moved to the Rockies so that she could wear mittens most of the year. Since 1996 she has tumbled around the Bow Valley and over the years has been fortunate to call spectacular places like Moraine Lake, Lake Louise, Banff, Sunshine Village, Jasper and Canmore her home. Jocey's illustrations can be found in all kinds of unusual places in the Bow Valley, as well as in her picture books *Nuptse and Lhotse Go to Iceland, Nuptse and Lhotse Go to the Rockies* and *Nuptse and Lhotse in Nepal*. She is currently working on two children's books that celebrate her love of this unique mountain landscape: an ABC Rockies board book and a 123 Rockies board book.

Barry Blanchard is the author of *The Calling: A Life Rocked by Mountains*. He is an internationally acclaimed mountain guide who has worked around the world. He lives in Canmore.

Ian Brown was the host of *Human Edge* and *The View from Here* on TVOntario for more than 20 years, and has hosted programming for CBC Radio One, including *Later the Same Day*, *Talking Books* and *Sunday Morning*. He has worked as a business writer at *Maclean's* and the *Financial Post*, a feature reporter for the *Globe and Mail* and a freelance journalist for other magazines, including *Saturday Night*. He is an occasional contributor to the American public radio program *This American Life*. Ian Brown has published four books, including *Freewheeling* (1989), about the Billes family, owners of Canadian Tire, and *Man Overboard*. *The Boy in the Moon: A Father's Search for His Disabled Son*, a book-length version of Brown's series of *Globe and Mail* features dealing with his son Walker's rare genetic disorder, Cardiofaciocutaneous Syndrome (CFC), was published in the fall of 2009. Ian Brown's newest book is *Sixty: The Beginning of the End, or the End of the Beginning? A Diary of My Sixty-First Year*

(2015). Brown began keeping a diary with a Facebook post on the morning of February 4, 2014, his 60th birthday. As well as keeping a running tally on how he survived the year, Brown explored what being 60 means physically, psychologically and intellectually.

Kristy Davison co-founded *Highline Magazine* in 2008, motivated by the pursuit of stories that both inspire mountain people and make us laugh at our weird, wild ways. Her background in fine arts and design (a BFA in photographic arts from ACAD and a design diploma from MRU), voracious appetite for reading and research and a life spent wandering in the Rockies combined to lead the vision and voice of the magazine.

Colette Derworiz is a senior staff reporter for the *Calgary Herald*, writing stories about the environment in southern Alberta. She has worked as a journalist at the *Herald* for more than 17 years, covering a variety of topics: education, municipal politics, health and social issues. In 2005 Derworiz won a National Newspaper Award for political reporting with a colleague for a special investigation into a civic election scandal. She was also part of a team that won another NNA for breaking news after its coverage of the Alberta floods in 2013. She spends much of her free time outdoors: hiking, biking and skiing. Derworiz lives in Canmore, where she can make the most of mountain life every day.

Ben Gadd is one of Canada's better-known naturalists and Rockies writers. Author of the groundbreaking *Handbook of the Canadian Rockies*, Ben has written or co-authored nine other books. His novel, *Raven's End,* has become a prize-winning Canadian bestseller. Ben has received four Banff Mountain Festival awards for his work, as well as the festival's prestigious Summit of Excellence. In 2009, after 29 years in Jasper, Ben and his wife, Cia, moved to the Bow Valley to be Grandpa and Grandma across the yard from Marie and Rose in Canmore.

Jamey Glasnovic was born in Montreal in 1968 and grew up in the suburb of Beaconsfield. He moved west in the mid-'90s and settled in Canmore in 2004. As a freelance writer and photographer, he has contributed to the *Canmore Leader*, the Banff *Crag & Canyon*, the *Rocky Mountain Outlook* and the *Independent* in the UK. Online, his work has appeared in *SolaraLife*. His first book, *Lost and Found: Adrift in the Canadian Rockies,* explores his connection to the Bow Valley and the surrounding Rocky Mountains parks system, and examines his sometimes awkward attempt at making this place his own.

Katherine Govier's tenth novel, *The Three Sisters Bar and Hotel*, is set in a fictional town called Gateway, at the edge of the Rock Mountain Park. Her previous novel, *The Ghost Brush*, about the daughter of the famous Japanese printmaker, Hokusai, creator of *The Great Wave*, appeared in translation in seven countries, including Japan. Her novel, *Creation*, about John James Audubon in Labrador, was a *New York Times* Notable Book of the Year in 2003. She divides her time between Canmore and Toronto.

In the winter of 2006, **Maria Gregorish** made her way to Canada, in search of new opportunities, adventure and a fresh start. Born in Romania, she had lived there during the Communist era and had experienced both the chaos and hopefulness of the revolution. When that hope faded into disappointment, she began searching for a new place she could call "home" and found it in Alberta's Bow Valley. Her writing interests include young adult fiction, in which she incorporates elements of Romanian mysticism, folklore and history.

Miki Kawano is a Banff-based high school student and writer.

Frances Klatzel is at home in the Bow Valley and the Himalaya. After a biology degree, she worked for Parks Canada for seven years. Her first trip to Nepal was to see the Himalaya, but the people and cultures of this diverse land compelled her to stay for many of the past 35 years in Nepal. All of her work there has utilized her skills in writing, photography and interviewing for oral history, and her knowledge of natural history and Himalayan cultures, especially the Sherpas of the Everest region. Frances maintains deep roots, family ties and friendships in the Bow Valley in a dual existence between two special mountain regions. While working for development projects and fundraising for various worthy causes, she started wondering how to help those left out from conventional assistance. Ten years ago, she co-founded a non-profit organization, CORE International, to pursue this goal.

Michale Lang has been a writer and curator for more than 25 years. She came to Banff in 2007 as the executive director and chief curator at the Whyte Museum of the Canadian Rockies. While in this role, she wrote and curated the Whyte's permanent exhibition, *Gateway to the Rockies*. Her publications include the children's book *Mary Schäffer's Adventures in the Canadian Rockies*, *An Adventurous Woman Abroad: The Selected Lantern Slides of Mary T.S. Schäffer*, *Yellowstone to Yukon: The Journey of Wildlife and Art* (co-author) and *Bears: Tracks through Time*. For three years, she did a weekly column on CBC's *Wildrose Country* about Alberta's mavericks. In 2008 Michale was a Woman of Vision Award recipient, recognizing her work in the cultural sector. Having lived in Field, BC, for more than 13 years in the 1970s and '80s, with Banff as her service centre and cultural hub, she has a long relationship with the Bow Valley.

Stephen Legault is a full-time conservationist, writer and photographer. He is the author of 12 books, including *Earth and Sky: Photographs and Stories from Montana and Alberta* and *Running Toward Stillness*. He lives with his sons, Rio and Silas, and wife, Jenn, in Canmore, in the dell of the Bow River.

Harvey Locke is a conservationist, writer and photographer who lives in Banff National Park. His family came to the Bow Valley when there were wild herds of buffalo, before the coming of railways or roads. His work has been published in many countries and he has received many awards, including the J.B. Harkin Medal for Conservation from the Canadian Parks and Wilderness Society and the Fred M. Packard International Parks Merit Award from the

International Union for the Conservation of Nature. He is co-founder of the Yellowstone to Yukon Conservation Initiative and of the Nature Needs Half Movement and is currently working on a book on the *World's Great National Parks and Their Landscapes*.

Dustin Lynx is the author of *Hiking Canada's Great Divide Trail*. He lives in Canmore with his family, where he can be close to the trails he loves. Recently, he started a publishing company called Imaginary Mountain Surveyors, which had one book shortlisted for the Mountain Fiction and Poetry Award at the Banff Mountain Film and Book Festival in 2013 and another that won the prize in 2014. Hiking is a lifelong passion for Dustin; writing and publishing are a couple of ways that he has found to share that inspiration with others.

Since arriving in the Canadian Rockies from Montreal in the early 1980s, **Lynn Martel** has established herself as a prominent and prolific voice for the Bow Valley mountain community. Author of *Expedition to the Edge: Stories of Worldwide Adventure* and *Tales and Trails: Adventures for Everyone in the Canadian Rockies*, both published by Rocky Mountain Books, Lynn has also written nine biographical booklets on prominent Rockies mountaineers for the Alpine Club of Canada. A passionate explorer of the backcountry by skis, boots and camera, Lynn writes regularly for the Bow Valley's own *Rocky Mountain Outlook*, *Highline Magazine* and Crowfoot Media, as well as numerous other publications and organizations. Through her intimate knowledge and deep participation in the Rockies' unique mountain culture, her stories recognize and celebrate the region's outdoor adventurers, historical figures, social issues, current events, natural world, environmental scientists and mountain-inspired artists, writers, filmmakers, photographers and personalities.

Joleen Brewster Niehaus is a sixth-generation Banff National Park resident who was born and raised in the Bow Valley. At the time of publication of *Imagine This Valley,* she was attending Banff Community High School and had aspirations of attending post-secondary school to study business so she might one day run her family's operations at Shadow Lake Lodge and MountView Barbecue. In her spare time, she likes to hike and enjoy the mountains of Banff National Park.

The Bow Valley has been part of **Ruth Oltmann**'s life since 1970, when she arrived to run a hostel for the summer. She's never left, and has worked at a variety of interesting jobs between the Bow Valley and the Kananaskis Valley. While running Ribbon Creek Hostel in Kananaskis, she started working part-time at the University of Calgary's Barrier Lake research station. There, she was asked to write a chapter on the human history of the Kananaskis Valley for a pilot study called *Man and the Biosphere.* That writing project ultimately became her first book, *The Valley of Rumours ... the Kananaskis.* Twenty years later, she published *My Valley the Kananaskis.* Her writing has included a small book called *The Kananaskis Valley Hikers and X-C Skiers Guide; Lizzie Rummel: Baroness of the Canadian Rockies,* a biography of an exceptional mountain lady; and *Ruthie's Trails*, a compilation of personal stories. Ruth's interest and work on the history of Kananaskis has led to speaking engagements, historical slide shows, a few magazine articles and teaching Elderhostel programs. She lives in the Bow Valley, in Exshaw.

Carol Picard is a transplanted prairie girl and 25-year resident of the valley, where she arrived in 1991, vowing to ski, hike and stay but a year. A former editor of both the *Canmore Leader* and the *Rocky Mountain Outlook,* and founder of the latter, she finds herself still here – a very common story in the Bow Valley. At 39, having almost escaped the last gasps of maternal urges, she succumbed and produced her finest legacy, the amazing Samantha Wendy Wade – currently studying acting in Vancouver. An avid reader and folkie, she's currently working on the Great Canadian Mystery Novel, in between bouts of extreme volunteer commitment to this wondrous community called Canmore.

Graeme Pole has published more than a dozen books and has been writing about the human history and the natural history of Western Canada for 30 years. He lives with his family near Hazelton, in northwestern BC, where he serves as a paramedic. Please visit his website: mountainvision.ca.

John Reilly was appointed to the bench at age 30 and had the distinction of being the youngest Provincial Court judge in Alberta history. At age 50, he made a promise to himself that he was going to improve the delivery of justice to the Stoney Nakoda First Nation at Morley, Alberta. After 35 years in public service, Reilly retired in 2011. He lives in Canmore.

Bob Sandford is the EPCOR Chair for Water and Climate Security at the United Nations University Institute for Water, Environment and Health and the co-author of the UN *Water in the World We Want* report on post-2015 global sustainable development goals related to water. In his work, Bob is committed to translating scientific research outcomes into language decision makers can use to craft timely and meaningful public policy and to bringing international example to bear on local water issues. Among many other appointments, Bob is also senior advisor on water issues for the Interaction Council, a global public policy forum composed of more than 30 former heads of state, including former Canadian Prime Minister Jean Chrétien, former US President Bill Clinton and former prime minister of Norway, Gro Brundtland. In addition to many other books, Bob is also the author or co-author of a number of high-profile works on water. His most recent book, *Storm Warning: Water and Climate Security in a Changing World*, was published in the fall of 2015.

Margo Talbot is a writer, speaker and climber based in Canmore. Although her passion is ice climbing, she enjoys all sports that get her out into the wilderness that surrounds the Bow Valley. Margo's love of cold, remote environments has taken her from the High Arctic to Antarctica, and the mountain ranges in between. She is the author of *All That Glitters: A Climber's Journey through Addiction and Depression*, a story that largely takes place amid the Rocky Mountains of Canada. As a keynote speaker, Margo has given presentations of her adventures in Canada, the United States and Australia. Her TEDx Talk, "Climbing Out of Addiction and

Depression," has had over 60,000 views as of June 2016. Her twin goals are to visit the remaining wilderness of the planet and share her story of healing and redemption.

Kevin Van Tighem has written more than 200 articles, stories and essays on conservation and wildlife, which have garnered him many awards, including Western Magazine Awards, Outdoor Writers of Canada book and magazine awards and the Journey Award for Fiction. He is the author of *Bears: Without Fear*, *The Homeward Wolf* and *Heart Waters: Sources of the Bow*.

Jon Whyte was the curator of Banff Heritage Homes, a foundation agency of the Whyte Museum of the Canadian Rockies in Banff. A poet, columnist, writer and filmmaker, Jon wrote several books and contributed to many anthologies, magazines and other media. He died in 1992.